To Peter

About the Author

JEAN PAIN is a psychotherapist in private practice. She holds a diploma in hypnosis and psychotherapy and is a Master Practitioner in NLP.

After taking an honours degree in Spanish at Liverpool University, Jean married and went to live with her husband in Venezuela where her two sons were born. On returning to England, she taught mathematics for five years. After that she started her own business and later opened a successful antiquarian and secondhand bookshop in the heart of Cambridge.

Jean's interest in human behaviour began when she was a small child and found herself at odds with most grown-ups. She was always aware that what people said and how they expressed themselves was often incompatible with what they really meant and how they behaved. This insight led to a life-long interest in any writer who examined or questioned the phenomenon.

After discovering the enormous potential of hypnosis and neuro-linguistic programming ten years ago, Jean trained and became a qualified psychotherapist.

In addition to running a successful private practice, Jean consulted at Champneys Health Resort for a number of years before leaving to complete an MA in practitioner skills at Manchester Metropolitan University.

Jean has three children and three grandsons and lives in Cambridgeshire.

So you want
to be a
Therapist

by

JEAN PAIN

DISCOVERY BOOKS

First published in 2000 by Discovery Books
29 Hacketts Lane Pyrford Woking
Surrey GU22 8PP

©Jean Pain 2000

Jean Pain asserts the moral right to be identified as the author of this work

A CIP catalogue record for this book is available from the British Library.

ISBN 0 9518511 4 4

Page and cover design by David Simpson
Cover drawing by Jean Pain
Printed by Professional Books Supplies Limited,
Abingdon, Oxon, UK
Cover printed by KMS Litho, Banbury, Oxon, UK.

Contents

Contents

Contents

Acknowledgments

Many of my acknowledgments are to the dead – (who says there is no immortality?) To Ludwig van Beethoven who taught me that beauty can be created from pain, during the most unhappy time in my life, my transition years from child to adult. To those tough, authoritarian teachers who took a strong line with me at school, gave me no sympathy and insisted upon my striving to do my best work at all times. To dear Sigmund Freud and Carl Gustav Jung who, at the age of eighteen, spoke to me of wonders I had never dreamt of and finally helped me to make sense of my life. To all those other writers who have helped to shape my thinking and given me encouragement that life is worth living and that our fate is in our own hands.

Acknowledgments to those who have helped me think more clearly and develop my skills, include thanks to my excellent teachers in neuro-linguistic programming and hypnosis, Sensory Systems and the National College of Hypnosis and Psychotherapy; to my brilliant teacher, Robin Child, who teaches so much more than painting; to all those people who have sought my professional help over the last seven years and have taught me at least as much as I have taught them; to my publisher, Catherine Beattie, for her unfailing belief in my work; to my family, who have always given me support and put up with my obsession with my work.

Foreword

I love my life. Every day I wake early with a sense of anticipation of the unknown. Every day is unpredictable with fresh challenges and something new to learn. My work-time is divided between seeing clients, writing and painting. Each activity stretches me to my limits and requires immense concentration, mental and emotional toughness as well as an ability to tolerate chaos and frustration. Running through the gamut of my feelings and emotions gives me the sensation of being intensely alive.

This work is my fourth career. I am on the threshold of my seventieth birthday. and have been practising for seven years. I hope to continue for another twenty.

This book is for anyone who is considering psychotherapy or counselling as a profession. Like all worthwhile under-takings, it has to be done for the right reasons. If your motives are right, you will love the work and never tire of it, for its variety is endless. You will thrive on the work , despite the frustrations and difficulties. These are what make your successes so spectacularly satisfying. On the other hand, if the work does not suit you, or you are not drawn to it by a powerful compunction, you will hate it and it will wear you out.

I use the term 'therapist' throughout this book as a shortened form of 'psychotherapist'. It applies to trained practitioners who deal with psychological problems in many different areas. All share one important underlying assumption – that body and mind interact with each other.

Because the book is based on my own experience as a practising therapist, I have used the female gender for the therapist and the male gender for the client, to avoid writing 'his/her' and 'he/she' on every page. When writing about therapists and clients generally, the impersonal plural is used. Like all reasonable people, my aim is to avoid giving unnecessary offence to anyone.

More people than ever before are seeking psychological help for their problems. This has led to a huge increase in the number of people wanting to train as therapists, but who often have little idea of what this entails. By sharing my experiences after seven years in private practice, I hope to clarify what it takes to be a therapist and how it feels to be engaged in this work.

Whatever kind of work we do, it should affect us positively and help with our personal development and satisfaction. Only then will we do good work.

Jean Pain

Introduction

There's a big difference between liking the idea of taking up a new career and actually doing it. Every year thousands of people fail to complete study courses or give up new jobs because they do not meet their expectations. Others enjoy training but afterwards have difficulty putting their newly-gained knowledge into practice.

This book aims to give the 'would-be' counsellor or psychotherapist an insight into what it is like to work as a therapist. As it is based on my personal experience and training, both prospective and working therapists will find much to relate to .

Naturally, I have been influenced by my life experience, extensive reading and formal training, both in neuro-linguistic programming and the use of hypnosis in psychotherapy. Nevertheless, I believe that whatever the personal orientation of the therapist, the basic principles for effective practice remain the same.

My previous book, *So you think you need Therapy,* gave an overview of what psychotherapy is all about and why it may be needed. It explored the differences and similarities between the various kinds of 'talking therapies'. This book takes this understanding a stage further. It helps the prospective counsellor or psychotherapist ascertain their suitability for this type of work and examines motives for wanting to join the profession.

The topics covered include counselling and therapy work from the psychotherapist's point of view, the problem of hidden agendas, and assessing the client's overall situation to decide what type of therapy to use.

Newly qualified counsellors and therapists often feel at a

11

loss when they begin practising. However much they have learned on their courses, it is quite daunting to take responsibility for therapy sessions. This book boosts the new therapist's confidence by suggesting strategies for opening and closing sessions and dealing with any difficulties that arise. The fear of being unable to help the client enough is a common emotion and is dealt with in some depth.

Therapists need to feel confident to inspire confidence in their clients. They take the lead and yet at the same time must follow clients and recognise the importance of their wishes. Getting the balance right takes considerable practice. and different ways to achieve this are described.

I hope all new and potential therapists will find this book a useful and practical guide to what it is like to be fully involved in the everyday business of doing therapy.

Chapter One

The fantasy and the reality

What is psychotherapy?

Psyche is the Greek word for the soul, spirit or mind.

Therapy is the prevention or treatment of disease.

Disease means a lack of ease or illness.

Ease means calmness, relaxation, lack of conflict and freedom from pain.

Psychotherapy means the prevention or treatment of illness of the mind, spirit or soul.

Why do you want to be a psychotherapist?

People want to become therapists for many different reasons, and the decision to pursue a career in this profession is not to be taken lightly. Every year, more new training courses are organised, while the number of people feeling depressed or otherwise unsatisfied with their lives also increases. Demand for trained therapists has never been higher.

If you are seriously considering becoming a counsellor or therapist, it is wise to explore the validity of your motives and gain a clearer picture of what is involved in the business of doing therapy.

Reasons why people want to be therapists

1. They believe they want to help others.

2. They think they have what it takes because people tell them their troubles.

3. They believe helping other people will make them feel good.

4. They like the idea of the status attached to being a helper.

5. They like the idea of having the power to help others.

6. There is no retirement age;

   it is a profession where it can be helpful to be older.

7. They think listening to other people's problems.is easy.

8. The money is good.

9. They can work from home.

10. They can be self-employed.

11. They want to understand more about what makes people tick.

12. They like studying and want to learn more about psychology.

13. They want to understand themselves better.

Check your own motives against this list. With so many positive assumptions it is hardly surprising that so many people like the idea of becoming a therapist. The only reason listed which is completely invalid is number 7: Listening to other people's problems is not easy. Intense concentration is required and there is much more to doing therapy than merely listening.

The desire to help others *(numbers 1-3)*
Wanting to help others sounds good – merely saying the words can give a glow of self-righteousness. However,

because there are many underlying reasons for wanting to help, you must be sure of your motives. For example:

By helping others you can forget your own troubles. It is true that you can forget yourself whilst doing therapy. The therapist needs to be focused on her client to do good work. However, she must also be aware of her own reactions, as any of her own unresolved problems may get in the way of the work.

You like giving advice. This could mean you like having control over other people's lives, so if you like giving advice, beware! Therapy is about facilitation and helping the clients become clearer about what they really want so they can advise themselves.

By helping others you can sort out your own problems. Being a therapist can help you to become more aware of your own problems, but it is entirely inappropriate and unfair to use clients for your own ends. Any personal difficulties you encounter during working sessions should be discussed separately with your supervisor.

You want praise and validation from your clients. Clients sometimes take the good work done with a therapist for granted. A therapist who needs recognition can be vulnerable to manipulation by clients. She must be able to validate herself and be confident enough to know when she has done good work.

You think you have the ability to help. Being sympathetic is useful for family and friends but can be dangerous for a therapist. Sympathy is different from empathy, enabling the therapist to understand what the client is going through without joining in his suffering. It is inappropriate for a therapist to feel sorry for a client. Someone who enters easily into the emotional states of others must learn to control this tendency before considering therapy training.

Therapists must guard against being badly affected by the problems of their clients.

You readily sympathise with unhappy people. Few things in life are as rewarding as being of real help to someone else. However, we need to be absolutely clear about what helping really means. It is not helpful to do too much for clients as this encourages dependence, and in time they will resent you for it. Everyone feels good when they achieve a measure of independence. Therapists encourage this sense of independence in their clients, just as a wise parent does with a child. Indeed, therapy has been likened to parenting. This means giving enough, but not too much support, and being aware of the right time to begin to withdraw support.

The common belief, that you will make a good therapist if people often tell you their troubles, is a fallacy. It is not because you have some special quality that draws people to you, but because unhappy people tend to pour out their problems to anyone who will listen. Likewise in therapy, allowing clients to ramble on about all the bad things in their lives merely reinforces their negativity and is bad practice. It also exhausts the listener. At the end of a good session, both therapist and client should feel enhanced by the work.

Status *(number 4)*

If we are honest with ourselves - and honesty is the first essential for good therapy - we need to admit that we are all seduced by the idea of special status. We want to feel different; we want to feel valued. A therapist's reputation grows when other people recognise and appreciate how effective she is at what she does. Because it takes time to build up a good reputation, recognition only comes gradually.

Good therapists are recommended by their clients, although not as many as in other professions, as some people prefer not to admit they have 'had therapy'. Once they feel better they want to forget there was anything wrong. Often they are the most demanding of clients in the early stages, begging their therapist with tears, not to give up on them. When the work is done, they may walk off without a backward glance, never to be heard from again. A good therapist soon learns to view this behaviour as a compliment.

Because clients usually know very little about psychological theory, they tend to regard psychotherapists as 'experts'. However, if the therapist feels superior to her client she will not be able to work successfully. The therapist and client come together as two people on equal terms, with respect for each other. Each has a different role and the roles are complementary. Good results come from joint work, not by the therapist 'curing' her client.

Power (number 5)
The desire to have the power to help others must be examined carefully as it can be dangerous.

If you feel the need for power, it may be because you are not in control of your own life. Accepting that your own actions and reactions shape your future is empowering. Only by changing what you do and the way you live your life will the desired result be achieved. This means a life-long undertaking of working with and understanding yourself – a daunting task.

Rather than meet this challenge, some people try to change others. They force them to fit in with their own ideas of how they should be, instead of allowing them to decide for themselves. This is a serious and common misuse of power. Anyone in a position of influence must be absolutely sure they are free of this kind of motive. Only when people have freedom of choice, do they develop inner fulfilment which allows them to help others achieve the same.

Psychotherapy is a profession with the power to help people change their lives. This is a great responsibility. A therapist must always use her power scrupulously for the good of others and not just to satisfy her own ego.

The Advantage of Age *(number 6)*

Psychotherapy is a profession where to be older can be a real bonus, provided that you are someone who learns from mistakes – not everyone becomes wiser as they age. Clients often prefer someone mature, and feel more comfortable with a person who is one or even two generations older than themselves. Provided you keep your memory for cases and your health, most importantly your mental health and energy, you can keep going indefinitely. Some therapists work into their eighties and there are a few who continue into their nineties. Self-employed therapists do not have to retire unless they want to; reducing the number of clients they see is always an option.

Working from home *(number 9)*

Working from home has its difficulties and can be a lonely experience. If you have always gone out to work you may find it hard to adjust. On the other hand, working from home has many advantages, like saving time and wear and tear on yourself by not having to travel so much. Your therapy work can be dovetailed with other activities so that your day has plenty of variety. Sessions can be planned so you have time off when you need it. *(See Chapter Eight for more information.)*

Being Self-employed *(number 10)*

Being self-employed opens up areas of anxiety. It may sound fine to be your own boss, but the reality is that you need to plan ahead to ensure you have enough work. It is useful to plan financially for the times when you are away on holiday or sick, as no-one pays you then. It can be daunting to be fully responsible for your own work until you get used to it. *(See Chapter Eight for more information.)*

If you are self-employed, it is wise to check with an accountant exactly what you need to do to satisfy the requirements of the Inland Revenue and VAT office. Personally, I prefer to have my accounts done professionally. It may be more expensive but saves the worry of wondering whether I have done the right thing. My accountant also keeps me up to date with any new legislation that might affect me.

Money *(number 8)*

Yes, the money can be good. It all depends what you are comparing it with. For instance, people trained in NLP and working as business consultants earn considerably more than NLP therapists. There are also great variations in what people charge for therapy, as this depends on their training, location and fame.

However, when you are working well you are likely to be working harder than ever before. You may find ten to fifteen sessions a week is as much as you can manage without becoming overtired. Time is also needed to review clients' notes, to do extra research in unfamiliar areas and to ponder on ideas that occur to you between sessions. This extra time is not paid for.

Curiosity *(number 11)*

To be curious about other people's lives is essential. Every new client is like an unopened book – a new story we haven't heard before. We may have heard others like it, but none quite the same. It is this interest that gives you the stamina for the intense concentration proper listening demands. You are not only listening but also monitoring the client's body language and watching out for clues. You will then know the crucial time to intervene and ask questions or do some talking yourself.

Because there is so much emphasis on the importance of listening, it is an easy mistake to assume that a therapist is not allowed any input. There are many ways of using language and telling stories which are useful to the client. The important thing to remember is to keep your attention focused on the client's needs and not on your own.

Understanding yourself better (number 13)

The desire to know yourself better is essential if you want to be a therapist. As your understanding of yourself increases, so does your willingness to accept yourself as you really are. You are prepared to acknowledge the things you cannot change and to work at changing those you can. Working on yourself makes you more tolerant, patient and helpful to those people who choose to work with you. Always remember that the therapist's first consideration is the client's well-being. While she inevitably develops herself in the course of her work, her own personal psyche should be explored with her own therapist, not with her client.

Getting qualifications (number 12)

Although no legal qualifications are needed to practise as a therapist, it is important to have some form of recognised training. *So you think you need therapy* gives an overview of what is available. In recent years there has been a huge proliferation of counselling and psychotherapy   courses in both the public and private sector. Many countries around the world now offer a variety of certificates and diplomas – from ten hour introductory courses to degree programmes lasting several years.

In the UK, details of training courses can be obtained from The United KIngdom Council for Psychotherapy (UKCP) and The British Association of Counselling. (BAC). The latter produce an annual directory *Training in Counselling and Psychotherapy* listing national training institutions and approved courses throughout the UK. *(See Appendix for addresses)*.

If you have not done any studying for a long time do not be put off. *(See Chapter Three for a brief overview of things that get in the way of learning and how you can overcome them.)*

If you enjoy learning new things and have a burning desire for a better understanding of human nature, you are already ahead. As always, motivation and determination are the two forces which empower your progress. If you give up too easily, then psychotherapy is not for you, as you need all your motivation and stamina once you have begun your practice.

Every good training course has its code of ethics and rightly so. It is not ethical for anyone to think they know best about another person. Therapists must remain open-minded and take into consideration their clients' wishes at all times. Always remember that however intuitive the therapists may be, they are not always right. Therapists are frequently surprised by clients they thought they had the measure of.

Reality and fantasy

To have the ability to visualise how things might be in a different situation is a useful skill. All entrepreneurs, designers and engineers need this ability. Without the dream we cannot achieve the reality. This book is intended to narrow the gap between your dream and the reality of becoming a psychotherapist.

Chapter Two

Liking the idea of doing something

- *enthusiasm and motivation*

- *procrastination and depression*

The early years of babyhood and childhood are the time in our lives when we feel motivated and enthusiastic, if we are encouraged, not forced, to develop our bodies and minds. Babies do not procrastinate about walking. Toddlers fall over repeatedly as they learn to co-ordinate the different muscle movements needed for balance with forward progression. All babies have the confidence that they will walk and each baby learns at his or her own pace.

Similarly, when we are small we all have favourite activities; games we prefer, music that attracts us, people we like to be with. We know how to please ourselves and have not yet learned to please other people. We have no difficulty knowing what we want to do. Ideally, we are surrounded by books, music and encouraging parents, who give us the chance to explore our environment as much as possible.

So what happens to our enthusiasm and motivation as we get older? Why do so many older children and adults lack confidence, procrastinate and have such difficulty in becoming motivated and enthusiastic?

One reason is because, at some stage, they have stopped pleasing themselves and are trying to fulfil other people's expectations. Too many "oughts, musts and shoulds" have crept into their thinking. and words like 'compulsory' have entered their vocabulary. Other factors that damp down our natural joy of life are the influences of misguided adults and the fact that as we get more familiar with the world, we begin to take it for granted.

Some people do keep their natural enthusiasm, never losing their joy at seeing the first rose of summer for example, and continuing to get intense pleasure from favourite activities. They are able to develop their creative powers in a positive way because, like small children, they do what they want to do and make personal development and their work their first priority. This is why creative people like writers, painters and musicians often live to a great age and continue to develop their work. Artists such as Jacques Villon, Matisse and Picasso produced some of their best work in their seventh and eighth decades. Such people are an inspiration, and show us that our later years can be even more rewarding than our earlier ones.

Origins of depression

Depression may occur when we fail to pay enough attention to our own needs, and try to fit into society by accepting its values too easily and without question. The proof of this is all around us – babies and young children brought up in a facilitating environment are rarely depressed, but the incidence of depression and dissatisfaction with life in the rest of the population is steadily growing due to the pressures of the times we live in.

Depression, difficulties in making relationships, lack of confidence and low self-esteem are the most usual reasons for people to seek therapy. The underlying common denominator in these problems is a weak sense of personal identity and not enough belief and confidence in personal talents and capabilities. Anyone considering becoming a therapist or counsellor and who is experiencing some or all of these difficulties, should tackle them first before working with clients. Indeed, many training schools now insist that student therapists undertake their own personal psychotherapy at the same time as they are working on their courses.

No-one is completely confident in every area of life and we all have negative thoughts and feelings about ourselves and our work from time to time. There are few people who would not benefit from some kind of psychotherapy. We all need to know ourselves better.

The way through

Ongoing therapy makes clients realise that the factors holding them back in life and preventing them from doing what they want, are usually related to their own false beliefs and faulty thinking. Once they admit this fact, they can no longer blame their situation on outside forces.

Other people's behaviour affects us only if we allow it to. No-one can 'make' us feel sad, unhappy or discouraged, we do it to ourselves in response to a situation. A person can learn to respond in any way they want, but the more they allow others to affect them, the more they relinquish their own power.

An important part of being a psychotherapist is helping clients become more self-assured and less open to being controlled by their environment. As Shakespeare wrote: "Our future lies not in the stars but in ourselves."

The person without problems does not exist. Part of the exhilaration of living is the challenge of finding solutions to setbacks and difficulties. If a person has everything they want, they quickly become bored and miserable. The biggest illusion is believing that money brings happiness. Money does not cure a person's inner problems, only the individual concerned can do that. However, everyone needs help at some time in life, and the right kind of psychotherapy will unravel the real source of dissatisfaction and also help the affected person to do something about it.

Most people cannot do this by themselves, however determined they may be. This is because they naturally avoid looking at the things that frighten them. Support is needed to help them confront these issues.

Liking the idea of doing something

Chapter One considers some of the reasons why people like the idea of being a counsellor or psychotherapist and the possible underlying motives for this desire. If these motives come from false beliefs and expectations, this quickly becomes apparent when the reality of doing takes over.

Being a psychotherapist or counsellor means responding to your clients in all kinds of disconcerting ways. It happens to everyone in the profession who cares about their work.

For example, when a client begins to have confidence and trust in his therapist, he becomes more open. He starts to release long-buried feelings which may include strong emotions and resentment. The therapist must be prepared for this or it will come as quite a shock. The therapist who had been protecting her image as a kind, helpful person may suddenly be knocked off her pedestal. She may be dismayed to find she is irritated by the client she is supposed to care for. It is important that she acknowledges these feelings and is mature enough not to let her own emotions get in the way of her work.

In *Client Centred Therapy* (1990), Carl Rogers stresses the importance of the therapist constantly monitoring his/her own responses. He illustrates how the therapist can be spontaneous while maintaining rapport with the client. The principles have something in common with the parent/child relationship. The therapist must be firmly in control while respecting and caring for the client.

Maintaining motivation and enthusiasm

Motivation comes from wanting to do something. Many people lose their motivation or find it harder to maintain, once they are well into a project. This happens to everyone at some stage in life. Starting a new job or venture is like a honeymoon – everything is so new and different. Then we settle down into the everyday business of living together and developing a relationship. If the relationship is good and we care enough about the other person, we do the necessary work to bring about the results we want. The same principle applies to therapy. Not all sessions go well, but a therapist perseveres if she cares enough about her work.

No-one knows what causes the client to change and the process can be startlingly sudden or a long, slow process. Change depends on the therapist's skill, the client's temperament, the strength of the rapport as well as the underlying problems and life situation of the client at the time of therapy.

The therapist's continuing interest in understanding human nature is also a strong motivator. This quality is a blessing when things get tough and she begins to wonder whether a particular client will ever succeed in doing the necessary work to bring about change.

Other powerful motivators are a love of challenges and a thirst for solving problems, although care must be taken when and how these ideas are communicated to the client.

A client should never be pushed into accepting a truth about himself before he is ready. Pressure from his therapist will certainly alienate him. However intuitive his therapist may be, she can never be absolutely certain that she is right. Clients frequently surprise their therapists.

Procrastination

Procrastination is both a hindrance and a help. When considering a new career, you may delay signing on for a training course until you have enough information about the job to assess its suitability. When you are seriously contemplating becoming a counsellor or psychotherapist, it may help to play devil's advocate with yourself (or a close friend) and think up all the reasons for not doing the training. This is good for natural optimists who might otherwise overlook any negative aspects. However, if you have a more pessimistic nature, your natural tendencies can be counteracted by stressing the positive points of training for a new profession.

Clients also procrastinate, often waiting until they are really desperate before seeking therapy This can help the therapist, as the more frustrated a client is, the more motivated he will be to do the necessary work to improve his uncomfortable state of mind.

Sometimes a client seems to be 'stuck' and it may be necessary to risk trying something new to alleviate the crisis. At other times, when the situation is not so urgent, it is probably advisable to delay finding the root cause of the trouble until the client feels stronger. Experience makes the decision easier, although the therapist has no way of knowing if she is right without hindsight. Therapists are allowed to make mistakes – they are human after all. However, nothing will be learned if they are not prepared to take a few risks.

Chapter Three

Different approaches to therapy

Tried and tested talking therapies

Psychotherapy is an umbrella term covering a huge range of different approaches and techniques. Its purpose is to help a person understand and solve problems in life that are causing them to feel unhappy or unfulfilled. Psychotherapy enables them to be more in control of their own life, by breaking destructive thought and behaviour patterns. Most forms of psychotherapy involve the client talking to a trained therapist, although a few use other means of expression such as art and dance movement therapies.

Psychotherapy and counselling are closely linked. The term 'counselling' was first used by Carl Rogers in America. As he was not medically qualified to practise in California, he had to call himself something other than a psychotherapist so he chose to be a counsellor. He developed his own methods which are highly developed today and depend on the close rapport between counsellor and client.

The boundary between counselling and psychotherapy has never been clearly defined and continues to be blurred. The terms are used interchangeably in some areas and distinguished in others. It is certainly true that the skills, approach and theoretical understanding of trained counsellors and psychotherapists overlap in many areas.

In the UK, counselling and psychotherapy training, have no clearly defined differences and similar skills are taught for both methods.

Two different approaches to psychotherapy

In psychotherapy, the therapist works from the outside to the inside or vice versa

If the therapist uses the outside (*behavioural*) approach, she works on the behaviour itself (the symptoms) and tries to remove their cause. Alternatively, she may take the inside (*psychodynamic*) approach and look for the underlying cause of the problem. When this is found and dealt with, the client's behaviour should change spontaneously

Of the two approaches, the behavioural one is easier to use as it requires no in-depth insight and techniques like visualisation can be used. It works from the outside to the inside.

The psychodynamic approach works directly on the underlying cause of the behaviour. It assumes that when the client understands and comes to terms with hidden and often long-standing traumas, his uncomfortable symptoms disappear and his attitude to life changes. The success of this approach depends on the therapist's intuition, imagination, and ability to 'get on the same wavelength' as the client. This is working from the inside to the outside. It requires a greater degree of skill than the behavioural approach because it works at much deeper levels of the human mind.

Phobias can be resolved by both approaches. A client who suffers panic attacks in enclosed spaces can be helped with de-sensitisation techniques. He faces his fear by going into the situation – initially with his imagination and then by actually doing what he fears. Alternatively, his problem may be overcome by uncovering the association between his present fears and past traumas. Both methods produce good results but the psychodynamic method is likely to have a more lasting effect. It is also possible to use parts of each method to achieve the best result. Habits are always hard to break even when we know why we have developed them, and it usually takes some time before change occurs. In such cases the behavioural approach can be helpful.

Some tried and tested therapies

■ Cognitive therapy

This popular therapy directly tackles clients' underlying thoughts, daydreams and attitudes by examining their language. There is a direct interchange between therapist and client, who is not encouraged to talk at length about his problems, but shown how his words reflect attitudes and influence behaviour. He is helped to change his language and the thinking behind it. By giving different meanings to experiences and recognising his power to change how he reacts to situations, the client learns to be more positive. The therapy includes homework between sessions and the client's progress is measured on charts. Cognitive therapy is a 'here and now' method. It may not take into account how the ways of thinking have come about.

■ Neuro-linguistic programming (NLP)

NLP has deservedly become popular because of its effectiveness in many fields, as a means of improving communication. It is used extensively in business training to build up confidence and show people how they can influence others and enhance their own performance. NLP appeals to both the scientific and arts-orientated person. Its positive approach is logically and clearly defined, as it uses both sides of the brain and all the senses, which are linked up in helpful ways

NLP tends to be thought of as a behavioural method, but also works psychodynamically. The client is led back through time to get in touch with earlier traumas. His therapist can then help him to experience his past differently, lessening the stranglehold of his fears and negating old traumas.

NLP works with astonishing speed when dealing with certain kinds of phobias and gives quick results for many other problems too. However, there are always cases where the process needs more time, whatever the techniques used. A successful outcome depends not only on the skill of the therapist, but on the nature of the problem and the character of the client.

Ericksonian hypnosis is an important part of NLP. Its success is due to its effectiveness in teaching communication skills at every level and in all areas of life.

■ Gestalt therapy

Gestalt therapy is based on the theory that all our needs are satisfied when we successfully complete the full cycle of our activities. For example, when we are bereaved, we need to work right through the experience and leave it behind. Gestalt therapy assumes that most of our ills are caused by unfinished business (uncompleted cycles from the past). The aim of the therapy is to discover exactly at what point in the cycle we become stuck.

The client who cannot give up mourning has not learned to let go; someone who overeats fails to recognise when he has had enough. Some people never start anything easily and have a problem with time in all areas of their lives. Others have difficulty in any situation that involves letting go of the past, so they hoard unwanted objects and cling to friends they would be better without. Whatever the situation, the cycle always remains uncompleted at the same point.

Gestalt therapy aims to complete these cycles of unfinished business. Role-playing is encouraged and the method includes a strong element of drama. It works well in groups where the participants are encouraged to interact.

Each person is helped and supported while exploring a painful past experience. It is a good method for shy people as it encourages them to come out of their shells.

■ Hypnosis

Hypnosis often gets a bad press. It is sometimes seen as a way of gaining power over others, so that they say and do things they would never ordinarily dream of doing. Another common fear is that hypnotised subjects may give away secrets whilst 'under the influence'.

These are the facts. Hypnosis is just one of many different trance states. We all experience trance states every day – from the bored child in class who never hears a word his teacher says as he stares out of the window, to anyone who 'loses himself' in a book, a television programme, a conversation or anything that absorbs the attention. We are all suggestible to ideas coming in from outside. The more imaginative and sensitive we are, the more easily we are affected. Meditation and prayer are other examples of trance states.

When we are 'entranced', our conscious minds have less control and the imagination (lodged in our unconscious mind), takes over. This is why we are easily influenced.

Hypnotherapy works well for addictions like smoking, nail-biting and over-eating. However, in the long-term it is only effective when the underlying reasons for the addictions are addressed. People become addicted because there is some unfulfilled need in their lives. Under hypnosis, mere suggestions alone are rarely enough to effect a long-term release from the addiction. We must really want to be free of the habit. A good hypnotherapist will take great pains to listen to the client and find out what it is he really needs and only *then,* use direct suggestions.

The so called 'false memory syndrome' has been given

much publicity. Some hypnotists were believed to have suggested or invented memories to their clients as they were undergoing treatment. These clients were then convinced that their 'memories' were real, causing them great distress. This should never happen. Hypnotherapists should always be ethical and never suggest ideas to their clients. Nor should they ask leading questions, which might make the client believe they have suffered a trauma such as sexual abuse, even when there are enough clues to think it is a possibility. A major factor in the success of any therapy is helping a disturbed person remember the traumas causing their discomfort. Symptoms often literally disappear overnight, once their source has been uncovered and dealt with.

Hypnosis is such an effective tool, that it is unfortunate that some people who could benefit from it are put off trying the therapy by bad publicity. Remember, any kind of therapy or medicine can be harmful in the hands of an ineffective or unscrupulous practitioner.

We are all capable of being sent into a trance by listening to the droning voice of someone making a boring speech. However, a therapist's attempts to hypnotise a client will only be successful if the client is co-operative. The essence of co-operation is trust, so it is important that the client feels comfortable and at ease. Hypnosis is a useful tool for the following reasons:

■ It helps the client relax his whole body, and increases the strength of the immune system.

■ It speeds up the building of self-confidence, making the client more aware of his natural talents and resources.

■ It enables the client to get in touch with buried feelings that need working through.

■ The negative effects of old traumas are overcome.

■ Natural creativity is enhanced, improving performance in areas of work and play where the client feels he could do better.

Hypnosis is especially effective when used at the end of a consultation to reinforce the work done in the session and to send the client away feeling good.

■ Client-centered therapy

Developed by Carl Rogers, this method is the basis of most counselling courses. It stresses the therapist/client relationship as the most important factor in successful work. The therapist must respect her client's wishes and realise that he knows best about his own needs. However, he may want help in discovering just what those needs are. Listening is considered vitally important. A client feels valued when he knows his therapist is fully concentrating on what he is saying. It helps to establish empathy.

■ Transactional analysis

Transactional analysis (TA) is more popular in America than in Europe. The method was developed by Dr Eric Berne who wrote the best-selling book *Games People Play*. The work revolves around the following theory:

In life we all play three roles, that of child, adult and parent. A properly mature relationship is based on adult speaking to adult. When we are in fear of authority, it is easy for us to go into child mode instead of maintaining our adult status. This makes us vulnerable to domination so that we cannot stand up for ourselves.

Through TA , the client learns to change the way he reacts in certain situations, so that he attracts a different response from other people and avoids being manipulated by them. TA believes that we create our life script in childhood from influences inside and around us. This is how we devise our own fate for the future. If this is an unhelpful one, TA can help us to change it for something more useful.

■ Eclectic therapy

This is the term for therapy that uses a mixture of different approaches. Some therapists prefer to use a combination of different therapies to help the client. This means the client receives 'custom-made' therapy, designed just for his needs. Since everyone is different, eclectic therapy makes good sense.

This list of therapies is by no means comprehensive. The psychotherapy umbrella covers too large and varied a range of therapies for them all to be described here. The ones in this chapter are some of the best-known, tried and tested kinds. They deserve their popularity because they have helped to change the lives of many people for the better.

Chapter Four

Psychotherapy Training

- *the choices*
- *what studying involves*
- *learning studying skills*

Choosing training

The kind of therapy you decide to pursue reflects your character and sense of identity. How you work and your individual style is determined by your temperament and personality.

When choosing a training establishment, keep in mind that each school of psychotherapy or counselling has a different focus. Some stress the relationship of the individual to the family and to society, while others give priority to events in the client's early life. Some schools emphasise the spiritual aspects of therapy, while others believe in working directly on changing behaviour. As in different religions, underlying common beliefs are shared by all psychotherapy teaching.

A great amount of research has been done to find out what makes for good therapy. Surprisingly, it seems that rapport – the relationship between therapist and client, is the key factor in determining whether or not therapy is successful.

Your choice of training does not prevent you from furthering your studies into different areas in the future. Many people do several kinds of training and most therapists continue attending workshops, conferences and seminars to broaden their general knowledge of the profession. The more training a therapist has, the greater her flexibility in treating her clients. In my own practice, I use NLP, gestalt therapy and hypnosis techniques, depending on the client and the situation.

The value of psychotherapy is now recognised by many psychiatrists, who formerly treated their patients' mental disorders with medication and behaviour therapy. Some doctors take post-graduate courses and become consultant psychotherapists.

Training in psychotherapy and counselling leading to a qualification is offered in both the state and private sector. Until recently, courses in psychotherapy, as distinct from psychiatry and psychology, were only available privately. Now that psychotherapy is recognised for its usefulness, more courses are available at colleges and universities. Good private training is still available, but tends to be expensive. This is probably because some colleges pride themselves on their reputation and experience in developing their courses. They want to ensure their training reaches the highest standards and continues to attract good students.

As a consumer, shop around and explore all the possibilities for training. Arm yourself with as many brochures as possible, visit the colleges and talk to the students and people who run the courses.

Approach to study

If you are taking up psychotherapy as a change of career or profession, the transition to studying should present no problems. However, many people who decide to train as counsellors or therapists have done little studying since they left school. This is particularly true of women who have dedicated themselves to bringing up their children and have not done demanding work outside the home for some years.

When you have decided where to train, you will be faced with the reality of getting down to serious study, a thought that probably fills you with apprehension. You may fear you will be unable to understand the books you must read, that you lack the necessary concentration or that your memory will not be good enough. You may even dread the thought of writing essays. Stop worrying, you are almost certainly exaggerating the difficulties. Remember that negative feelings and thoughts can actually prevent you from doing what you want.

It is a fact that the more you use your brain, the better it functions. You do not have to be an academic to train as a therapist. Anyone with experience of handling people, resolving difficulties successfully and making the most of their own relationships, already possesses useful skills. If you have always enjoyed reading, take an interest in what is going on in the world and love solving problems like crossword puzzles, your brain will be active and flexible and able to adapt well to studying. An independent spirit and plenty of common sense (which includes believing in your own abilities) will take you a long way.

Starting to read

The term 'technical book' applies to any non-fiction book about a specific subject, such as gardening, fishing, literary criticism, computers, or psychological theory. Whenever you take up a new interest you are immediately presented with a barrier of specialised language, or jargon. It is impossible to write a technical book without using jargon, but many could be better phrased in simple English.

When you start reading psychology books you will come

across new terms which may be alarming at first: "How will I ever understand all this?" Well, the journey of a thousand miles begins with the first step. Do not be put off. Arm yourself with a dictionary of psychological terms and be prepared to look up a particular word or phrase several times before assimilating its meaning. Be patient with yourself. Remember other times in life, when you started doing something new, like learning to drive, and think how easily you do it now.

Start by reading some self-help books. Two of the best are *Being Happy* and *Making Friends*, written and illustrated by Andrew Matthews. The cartoons encourage the reader to learn and laugh at the same time. You can then progress to the more heavyweight books. The bibliography at the end of this book lists some highly readable books which introduce psychological theory, and your tutor will almost certainly give you a reading list. If you find some of these books hard going, do not worry. In all probability, everyone else on your course will be having the same difficulty. If you compare notes with your fellow students, you will soon realise you are not the only one having problems.

Tips for tackling a new book

- First read the list of chapter headings and note any that are of particular interest to you.

- Read the introduction to find out the author's intentions.

- Read the first and last chapters to gain an overall view of what the book is about and what it is trying to say.

- Scan through the book, passing over anything you don't understand but stopping when you come across something that interests you. Don't worry if you cannot understand everything. Your concentration will be greatly improved if you focus only on the parts that fascinate you.

■ The following day, scan through the book again. You will be pleasantly surprised to find that much of it is familiar.

■ The next day, repeat this process and you will find that you understand more.

■ Begin to scan the difficult parts, without worrying and without trying to grasp them. Gradually extend the range of what you notice in the book and everything will become clearer.

■ After one week you will notice how much more you have understood and remembered. The secret of remembering is to go over the same material several times soon after reading it for the first time, allowing several hours or a day between reading sessions.

It is a great mistake to try to understand everything in a book. What really matters is how much you have taken in, not what you have left out.

Learning how psychotherapy has developed over the years adds an interesting new dimension to your studies and helps you to work more effectively. Reading about the lives of the great figures of the past and how they developed their theories increases your understanding. Unfortunately, in these modern times there is a tendency to discredit the work of people such as Freud and Jung. Some of their works are not easy to read, but the effort to do so is certainly worthwhile. Freud's *Jokes and their Relation to the Unconscious* is one of the fundamental works on the nature of creativity and is not too demanding on the reader. Jung's memoirs of his own life, *Memories, Dreams and Reflections* and his last book *Man and his Symbols* are fascinating. Anyone who is interested in the meaning of life could not fail to find them useful.

Writing essays

Some courses, though not all, require a certain number of essays to be produced. This is fine for students good at expressing their ideas clearly in a logical manner, but may be difficult for others. If this is a problem ask your tutors for advice, as some courses provide help in the writing of essays. In the meantime, here are some guidelines to consider:

■ Read the essay subject carefully and make sure you understand what is required.

■ Write in your own words how you have interpreted the ideas you have read.

■ Make sure your ideas progress logically so that one paragraph naturally leads on to the next.

■ As you get used to writing, so you will become more adept at selecting the most important facets of your argument and leaving out minor details.

■ Make sure you have a beginning, a middle and an end.

■ It is better to have more short sentences and fewer long ones.

■ Never use a complex word where a simple one will convey the same message. The best writing is simple and clear.

■ The easier your text can be read and understood, the better your writing.

■ Cut out all unnecessary words.

■ Jotting your ideas down on paper and revising them afterwards, is better than staring at a blank piece of paper

■ The more writing you do, the easier it becomes and the more skillful the writing.

Protecting the reputation of therapists

Because training and practice in the private sector is unregulated, some therapies have acquired a dubious reputation. As I have previously mentioned, hypnosis, one of the most useful tools for therapy work, has attracted much criticism in the media because of its misuse by some practitioners. Like all skills, it can be used for good or bad.

In many parts of the world, organisations and associations have been set up to protect the reputation of the profession of psychotherapy and the public, by promoting high standards of training, education and research. Some of these are listed in the Appendix on page 132.

In Britain, The United Kingdom Council for Psychotherapy (UKCP) has compiled a list of reputable practitioners of alternative methods as well as traditional psychiatrists, psychoanalysts and clinical psychologists. Only practitioners from training organisations considered to have reached a high enough standard are eligible to be included. The letters UKCP after a therapist's name mean that the public can have confidence in that person's training and qualifications.

The British Psychological Society is another professional organisation for other kinds of therapists. They accept only professionals with a psychology degree, which many psychotherapists do not have. Contrary to general belief, a degree in psychology does not provide the skills to do psychotherapy without further training. However, it is essential for certain careers, such as that of an educational psychologist, and in many parts of Europe and the US, you need a degree to practise.

Chapter Five

Finding a purpose in life

- *knowing yourself*
- *re-assessing your beliefs*

I believe that much of the unhappiness suffered today is because many people feel their lives have no meaning. It seems that human beings need to have a purpose which transcends their everyday lives. This contributes to the welfare of their fellow beings and enables them to feel part of a whole. Although some people are aware of this need from an early age, most are too busy studying, enjoying themselves and developing families and careers to consider exactly why they are doing these things. As we grow older, the need for a higher purpose in life gets stronger. Perhaps this is why increasing numbers of mature people want to do work in later life that involves being of use to others.

One way of thinking about your future life is to imagine that you are very old and quite prepared to die at any time. You are satisfied because you feel you have lived a worthwhile life. This is what creates feelings of contentment. However, many people find this visualisation difficult. You need a strong sense of your personal beliefs and identity to be clear about your aspirations

Who am I?

Shakespeare was very aware of our need to know ourselves:

This above all, to thine own self be true
And it must follow as the night the day
Thou cans't not then be false to any man.

However, not many people have a clear idea of their own character and spend their lives failing to satisfy their inner needs. We think we know what we want rather than what we need. Only when we want what we need, do we start moving in the right direction. The two biggest blocks to self-understanding are guilt and fear, which we feel acutely when we fail to live up to other people's expectations.

- We are afraid that if we do not do what others want, they will withdraw their love making us feel isolated and rejected.

- We may fear we would not have the strength to cope on our own, should we lose the support to which we are accustomed.

- We would then have to make our own decisions, which may further alienate family and friends.

- We may not trust our own judgement about ourselves and think that possibly other people are right in their estimation of us. Perhaps we do lack the ability to do the things we want.

These negative reactions are very common. If we were all brought up by wise and loving parents and teachers, we should be able to keep our natural sense of our own worth and learn to be fully independent. This means making our own decisions and being strong enough to withstand destructive criticism from outside and constructive criticism when we feel it is justified.

All children are naturally spontaneous in their behaviour

and have faith in their own judgement – they never fail to learn to walk, talk or ask for their needs to be met (provided that they are not mentally or physically handicapped).

Two of the greatest sins committed against children are causing them to feel fear and burdening them with guilt.

Guilt is an acceptable feeling when a person has deliberately done something to harm someone else. However, it is entirely inappropriate to feel guilty for not fulfilling other people's expectations.

Similarly, fear is a useful emotion when it acts as a cautionary brake on reckless behaviour, but harmful when it prevents us cultivating our talents. One of psychotherapy's most helpful aims is enabling people to understand who they are, and to differentiate between what they really believe and what they think they should believe

Reassessing our beliefs

Psychotherapists must be able to make these discriminations for themselves. They can only help others if they know what they believe and have confidence in their own decisions. This does not mean that they must always think they are right. On the contrary, they must change their beliefs when necessary and acknowledge that they sometimes make mistakes. Our beliefs do not usually remain constant throughout life. The effect of new experiences and learning causes us to change or modify our views.

Reflecting on our past mistakes and learning from them enables us to cope in the future. Unfortunately we appear to have a natural tendency to learn slowly from our mistakes or even not at all. The proof of this is the vast number of people who keep repeating patterns of unhelpful behaviour, such as finding new partners, all of whom resemble each other in fundamental ways.

Resentment and envy are two common human feelings that are usually accompanied by a tendency to blame everybody and everything, except one's self. Before we can begin to function effectively, we must be aware that the real enemy is within ourselves. Fortunately, most people seeking therapy treatment appreciate this. If not, they must become aware of it quickly or will fail to make progress.

Chapter Six

Practising therapy

Ways of working

There are many different ways of practising therapy. How these work in practice is fully explained in *Individual Therapy* edited by Windy Dryden (see bibliography). As the aim of all therapy is to assist the client, sessions are organised to meet individual needs. The following examples describe the most widely used working practices.

■ *One-to-one*

This is the most common arrangement. It is also the most expensive because the client has the therapist's exclusive attention. The therapist's role is that of facilitator and detective. Sadly, many people feel they have never had anyone's undivided attention at any time in their lives, something that is hard to believe, but true. They need help to become aware of their own needs and to identify the cause of their dissatisfaction. Occasionally, a client becomes self-indulgent and uses the sessions to unload negative baggage onto the therapist. A good therapist will not allow this to happen.

One-to-one therapy can be long or short term. It depends on the nature of the presenting problem and the client's personality and willingness to try new ideas, or may be a combination of both.

■ Group therapy

There are many ways of working in a group. Group therapy is used in psychiatric hospitals and 'drying-out' clinics as well as in private practice. It can be comforting for clients to have company in therapy: they realise they are not alone and that other people have difficulties too.

The success of group therapy depends on how well the people involved form a bond and most importantly, the personality of the therapist facilitating the group. This type of therapy is often more of a challenge to a therapist than one-to-one work. She must keep control of the group and have a sixth sense for when trouble is brewing — there is always a slight danger that one of the group may vent frustration on a more vulnerable member. Her role in group therapy is rather like that of a school teacher, watching out for trouble, leading and facilitating.

Psychodrama is a useful and enjoyable way of working in group situations, especially for clients who love acting and role-playing. It is most rewarding when shy, retiring people bring themselves to participate. Role-playing is a safe way to explore and practise new behaviour, and enables clients to become familiar with the new conduct before trying it out in real life.

■ Pairs counselling

Pairs counselling allows a couple to explore their relationship so that they understand themselves better and can express any false ideas they have about one another. When each partner becomes aware of how he or she is misunderstanding and distorting what the other is thinking, saying or doing, there is a chance that the relationship may develop and become more satisfying. However, there is also a risk that one or both parties may decide that separation is the best outcome. The counsellor is a facilitator, helping the pair reach their own conclusions. Married, unmarried and gay couples are all catered for in this kind of therapy.

■ Family counselling

It is now accepted that when a child has psychological problems it is essential to treat the whole family. The child's position in the family is also relevant. For instance, eldest and only children have characteristics in common, having been alone with the parents without the competition of brothers and sisters. It is believed that all children experience a sense of inferiority, before they develop their talents. Some are affected more than others as they strive to overcome negative doubts and develop feelings of personal worth.

A child's problems cannot be dealt with in isolation. They are an integral part of the family's behaviour patterns, which is why it is essential for the whole family to participate in the therapy.

Great skill is demanded on the therapist's part, to avoid a situation where blaming occurs. After several counselling sessions, the attitude of the parents and siblings slowly changes and this in turn gradually brings about a change of behaviour in the child experiencing difficulties. Successful family therapy leads to an improvement in the well-being, not only of the child but of the whole family.

■ Co-counselling

This is a relatively new kind of counselling. The facilitator sets up an arrangement in which the participants pair up and counsel each other, taking it in turns to be client and therapist. One person talks and the other listens for about half an hour, then they change roles. This gives the participants a feeling of mutual support as both are in the same position. and neither is a trained counsellor.

The disadvantage of this method is the participants' lack of training, although a good facilitator should be able to sort out any difficulties arising and encourage discussion.

Chapter Seven

The advantages of being older

- *how our brain functions*
- *it's never too late*

Young people face great challenges today. If they study hard and learn the new technologies they can earn high salaries and make fast progress up the careers ladder. However, youth is brief and they need to achieve their ambitions in their twenties or thirties. By the time they are forty, they may be considered too old, should they be made redundant and need another job at a similar high level. Many young high-flyers are burning themselves out with the constant pressure and demands of their employers. In the tough corporate world, their employers' very existence depends on keeping one step ahead in a rapidly developing and highly competitive market. Indeed, this is one reason behind the increased demand for therapists to work with stressed-out people.

Since we are all living longer, the next few decades will see an increase in the number of senior citizens. For most people, the age of retirement remains the same despite the fact that today's retirees are generally fitter than previous generations. Retirement is likely to be welcomed by those who did not enjoy work and now have time to develop their hobbies. However, individuals who love their work and feel part of society because of it, are likely to experience a loss of purpose and feel disoriented. This can lead to depression – and often does.

The psychotherapy profession plays its own part in turning the tide in favour of the older person, by showing that therapy is one job which does not impose a retirement age, and where it is a distinct advantage to be older. People who train as psychotherapists in their mature years have many advantages. They have survived life's trials and tribulations and experienced many of the problems they are likely to meet when dealing with clients. The more they have worked through past events and learned from them, the more they will be tolerant, patient and understanding of their clients' difficulties..

The ages of people who begin psychotherapy training ranges from the thirties up to the sixties or even the seventies. It is also possible, although unusual, for someone in their twenties to start the training. It all depends on the person concerned – there are always exceptional people who have many varied experiences early in life and reach a level of maturity and wisdom ahead of their chronological age, but they are rare.

Forgetfulness

Everyone is forgetful sometimes. The old stereotype of the absent-minded professor is a reality, not a joke. When you are capable of great concentration you pay little attention to the mundane practicalities of life. You find yourself mislaying keys and glasses because your thoughts are elsewhere. The more interesting your inner thoughts, the less attention you pay to everyday matters.

Forgetting names is a common complaint. There are various techniques you can learn that may help you to remember and they do work. The more you worry, the worse it becomes, so the answer is either to train yourself or to ignore it and hope for the best.

Forgetfulness is also a symptom of depression. People who have unconsciously blotted out large sections of their past, find to their surprise, that they are forgetful in other areas too. Once a person has learned the art of forgetting, albeit unconsciously, he may unknowingly extend it to other areas. It is a moot point whether anything is ever really forgotten. For instance, if you started to write your autobiography you would be amazed at how many events and dates you could remember.

Concentration

When people find concentration difficult, they are either not interested enough in what they are doing, or have an inner battle raging which is claiming all their attention. It seems that the more unresolved problems people have, the worse their concentration becomes for activities such as reading. When these problems are resolved, concentration returns.

Short attention span is another complaint of our times. When things are made too easy and we are not stretched mentally, we may fail to develop the ability to persist. However, we will always make the effort if we want something badly enough.

Making connections

One of the most important functions of the brain is to make connections – we could not even think if our brain cells did not connect. Every time we learn something new, another set of connections, known as a neural pathway, is created in the brain and a new habit formed. In no time, what seemed difficult at first becomes childishly easy, like walking and talking for example. The more you learn and have to struggle with problems, the greater the number of connections your brain will make. If you have used your brain well all your life, you will have more connections than most people. It may take you a little longer to retrieve the information, but once found, you will remember it well. You will also have an improved sense of priorities, so that you know what to discard and what to keep. This is important for many functions, especially writing. You only have to look at the lives of some of our most creative people to see that many have done their best work in late middle and old age. It is never too late.

Chapter Eight

Setting up as a therapist

Once her training is finished, several employment options are open to the newly qualified therapist wanting to practise. She can take a job, go into partnership with one or more colleagues or work by herself

Taking a job

Many organisations in both the public and private sectors, appreciate the value of having a part or full-time psychotherapist or counsellor on their staff. These include the social services and private consultancy companies who run assistance programmes and need qualified therapists to counsel employees from large companies.

Psychotherapy and counselling positions are advertised in several national newspapers and publications in the UK, including the *Guardian* (Tuesdays and Wednesdays), the *Independent* (Thursdays), *New Statesman and Society* (weekly) and the *Times Higher Educational Supplement* (weekly).

Going into partnership

Working in a practice with a colleague provides you with company and mutual support. Another possibility is to work within a group practice where several different kinds of therapy are practised. Clients are referred within the group when extra work of a different kind is needed, or when the client seeks a different kind of therapy altogether. The therapists share the costs of the premises and the salary of the receptionist, who arranges appointments and acts as a secretary.

One of the advantages of working in a group practice is that it acts as a magnet, drawing in more clients because of the wider choice. There is also more money available for joint advertising. A group practice encourages a mutually beneficial exchange of ideas, such as ways of attracting new clients and how different practitioners can co-operate for the well-being of all the clients using the practice. Working with like-minded colleagues also provides a sense of conviviality and companionship as well as the opportunity to discuss different aspects of work. Having a qualified medical practitioner in the practice is especially useful, as a medical diagnosis can be quickly provided when a client has symptoms which might be psychosomatic.

The downside of working with colleagues in a group practice is that conflicts caused by internal politics are fairly common. When taking on a new partner for the practice, all members should have the opportunity to voice their opinion as to the suitability of the candidate. When all the members of the practice are open-minded and tolerant, any differences that inevitably arise are resolved amicably. However, should a member put her own self-importance before the well-being of the group, this is likely to have a damaging effect on the practice.

Working on your own

Practising alone allows the therapist the freedom to please herself without consulting with someone else. All accredited therapists have a supervisor to help with any difficulties that arise in their work. Supervisors are experienced therapists who are prepared to discuss cases and offer help when needed. Most bodies that give accreditation make regular supervision a requirement for membership.

A therapist working on her own can decide to work from home. This has many advantages in the saving of time and money. Non-work activities can be done at the therapist's convenience, giving her the flexibility to do as many or as few sessions as she wants. Clients who are busy working during the day can be given out-of-office hours appointments. Working from home is great for therapists who dislike routine and prefer variety in their day.

Working from home is only an option if the home environment is conducive to the peace and quiet needed for clients. Practising from premises away from home helps to keep home and work separate. Some therapists operate from one small office, others work in three or more locations to build up practices in several areas, which may be necessary when full-time work is needed. Some people choose to work in London, where rooms can be rented for one or more specific days a week at prestigious addresses like Wimpole Street.

Self-employed therapists working alone or in a group practice are free to choose the clients they work with. When possible, it is always better to be selective, as with experience, you will soon recognise those cases which for one reason or another, you do not wish to take on.

Finding clients - advertising

If the right publication is chosen, advertising for clients can be quite effective. Unfortunately, advertising is expensive and one-off advertising is nearly always useless. Do not be persuaded to advertise in diaries printed for organisations unless you wish to make a donation to help them – it won't help you. Although there are a multitude of different alternative health directories, therapists rarely find that advertising in them brings in new clients. Similarly, advertising in the year books produced by the different training organisations will not yield floods of replies. A therapist may get as few as one or two new clients a year from each of these sources.

Useful places to advertise include the lifestyle pages of local newspapers and the *Yellow Pages* telephone directory. Almost every household has a copy and it is easy to look up the required service to find an instant choice of local names and addresses.

You may get referrals from counselling and psychotherapy professional bodies, once they have accepted you as a member. This is certainly a low cost way of raising your profile in your local area, but is not likely to result in more than a few new clients a year.

Another way of finding clients is to inform all the local medical practitioners and hospitals about your service. How this information is received depends on whether the doctors are sympathetic to alternative therapies. A clearly worded, well-designed leaflet can be posted to all the practices in your area and followed up a few days later with a telephone call (in case your carefully planned leaflet has been lost or thrown out). Many doctors now employ psychotherapists and counsellors in their surgeries for one or more days a week. These therapists work directly with their patients, a trend that is likely to increase in the future. If this idea appeals, it is worth making enquiries at doctors' surgeries in your own town. The pay may not be as good as in private practice, but the service provides an opportunity to gain valuable experience. One disadvantage is that you cannot choose the patients you work with.

It takes time to build up a practice, so do not be discouraged if clients are scarce at first. Once you have done good work with a few clients, word will get around and you will start gaining new clients through recommendations.

It is also worth considering giving talks about your work to local groups like the Women's Institute. Local newspapers usually carry details of forthcoming meetings and contact phone numbers. Remember, all publicity is helpful when building up your practice and reputation.

Specialising

After practising for some time and settling into the routine of the work, most therapists find that they prefer some types of cases to others. It is interesting to note that therapists are often drawn to clients with similar problems to the ones they themselves have faced and overcome. Thus a therapist who has suffered a certain kind of abuse in childhood may find that she takes on more than her fair share of similar abuse cases.

All psychotherapists and counsellors discover certain types of cases that they do not wish to take on, either because they feel they have had insufficient training or because for one reason or another they do not want to deal with them. Sometimes the way a person speaks over the phone gives a therapist an uneasy feeling, and if this happens, I believe it is best not to work with that person. Therapists must feel confident from the outset about the relationship they have with their clients.

Some therapists want to specialise from the outset. For instance, if they are interested in working with couples, they may train with an organisation like Relate which specialises in pairs work. However, most therapists start off working with one client at a time. When they have had some experience they may then diversify into pairs counselling, group work or family therapy. The longer a therapist practises, the more she becomes aware of her personal preferences and special skills. Hands-on experience is the best and only way of discovering your own particular gifts for the job.

Chapter Nine

I don't know what I want to do

"I'm 70 years of age and don't know what I want to do when I grow up," confessed a well-read and cultured gentleman three years before he died. An accomplished raconteur, witty and good company, he had made an abortive attempt as a novelist and wrote poems for his friends. His manners were impeccable. Strange that such a talented and charming man could be satisfied drifting through life in an aimless manner. Did he never suffer frustration at not developing his writing, never reaching the wider market, never gaining the acclaim he would have revelled in? Apparently not. Yet still, there was that cry from the heart. "I don't know what to do when I grow up."

Therapists often hear statements like this from their clients. Many people are not particularly happy in their work but they do not know what else to do. In my own work, I am particularly interested in mid-life crises and use a form of expanded careers counselling to help clients look at their whole life, including their long-term aspirations and early enthusiasms.

In the long run, I believe people do what they want to do, however much they may protest otherwise. Unfortunately, what a person thinks they want, very often does not satisfy them when they get it. A man may devote himself to building up a big business perhaps because he wants money, fame, power or because he enjoys doing it. To his surprise, he finds himself feeling needy and dissatisfied once he has achieved his ambition. At this point he may actively seek further challenges in his life, or conversely, may find his need for them has waned and that he regrets not spending more time with his family and friends. He may have spent many years of his life working hard, without thinking about his life's purpose, only to find that having achieved his goal it has turned into fool's gold in his hands.

There are doctors who want to be entertainers, factory owners who yearn to give everything up and cultivate their gardens, career women who regret not having spent more time with their children, and mothers who feel empty and unhappy when their chicks have flown the nest. All these types of people and many others seek therapy to discover what it is they really want and how they can get it.

When I work with my own clients, I usually start by asking them to write a list of all the things that gave them pleasure when they were children. I am always amazed at how few people can remember. (A poor memory for childhood events may indicate a considerable degree of buried childhood unhappiness.) Fortunately, techniques such as hypnosis and visualisation can be used to bring back forgotten memories, when this appears to be necessary.

Once the client has touched upon his early interests we can begin to chart the possible causes of his current distress. What was it that was so exciting, but was never followed up? Did the beloved piano practice have to end due to the pressure of exams? Did the client reluctantly take up the legal profession because 'art doesn't pay'?

Priorities

A client's priorities must be sorted out and tough questions asked and answered. For example, is he prepared to give up a lucrative career for the sake of doing something that will be more satisfying? If the answer is no, then tough – he cannot have his cake and eat it. If he decides that money and influence come before the satisfaction of his inner hunger and frustration, that is his choice. He may offer excuses disguised as reasons which all begin with the words "If only".

"If only I didn't have the children's school fees to pay."
(He does not have to pay school fees. His children do not have to be educated privately and will not necessarily benefit.)

"If only there were someone else who could take over from me at work."
(If he becomes ill through overwork, which seems quite likely since he is working so hard, someone else will have to do his work. No-one is indispensable.)

"If only I could be sure that things will work out well."
(There are no guarantees in life. No-one can be sure how things will turn out. Unless he is prepared to take risks he will never get his heart's desire.)

Chapter Ten

New clients

Taking on a New Client

When a new client rings up for a first consultation, I do not get out my appointments book immediately. I ask a few questions to find out about the person and the problem. This helps me to decide whether this is someone I could work with. My aim is to impress on the possible client, that whilst I am a good facilitator with a high success rate, I cannot do the changework for them. The task will be a collaborative one requiring hard work by both of us – client and therapist.

On one occasion, a caller became quite annoyed and said "You aren't convincing me that I should come to see you." To which I replied "That's right. I'm not trying to." I want my clients to come of their own free will, knowing what therapy entails. Only then is it likely to be successful. When I first started practising, I took on anyone who wanted to come. Now I am more selective and get better results.

How many sessions?

The number of sessions likely to be needed depends on the three factors mentioned previously, namely, the personalities of the therapist and client and the problem itself.

Generally speaking, problems arising from childhood traumas and reinforced over a long period, are not resolved quickly. In such cases, the character of the client usually determines the number of sessions. Someone who is optimistic and a natural fighter recovers quicker than a pessimist who sees himself as a victim.

Short-term Clients

These clients need brief therapy, often less than five sessions, to sort out their problems. Some arrive in a state of confusion, unable to understand what is bothering them. Their thinking and reasoning skills are in a muddle and they are extremely frustrated.

Using a combination of cognitive therapy and neuro-linguistic programming (NLP) is often helpful in such cases. Establishing a good rapport with the therapist soon clarifies their thinking, so that they view things differently. Experiencing frustration and exasperation is undoubtedly the best motivator for seeking help and making changes.

Other clients arrive with habits they want to break, such as phobias, nail-biting and smoking. If the habit relieves no underlying anxieties and worries, the judicious use of hypnosis will give quick results. However, if the habit has hidden reasons that are not uncovered and dealt with, its loss will not be permanent.

Some people seek therapy because they have no-one to talk to and need a sounding-board. They fear they are going mad and want to talk about their behaviour. They ask if what they are experiencing is normal or unusual. They usually have little knowledge or insight into the complexity of human behaviour and relationships, and are often. helped by being recommended useful books to read.

A therapist's training includes knowing the difference between psychosis (insanity or serious mental illness) and neurosis (emotional affliction). If you find yourself out of your depth, refer your client to his doctor who can arrange for him to see a psychiatrist. Alternatively you may know of a colleague with specialist knowledge who can help him more than you.

Medium-Term Clients

Most clients require between five and twenty sessions with ten sessions being the average number. Clients suffer a wide range of difficulties, include specific phobias, like a fear of flying or wasps, which can usually be cleared up in a single session. The most common problems are lack of confidence, shyness, relationship difficulties and marital disharmony.

Medium-term clients arrive with certain expectations and conditions. They often do not want to go into their childhood experiences more than necessary. They expect you to do something to relieve their symptoms so that they feel more comfortable.

When their unhappiness is caused by a life situation such as the death of a special person or too much pressure at work, they need your support. This is best dealt with by understanding and a common-sense exploration of ways in which they can learn to cope.

Clients who are stressed at work are often in jobs they are not suited to - they are round pegs in square holes. They need help to examine their skills and temperament so that they can discover the type of work that will be rewarding and satisfying for them. In other words they may need careers guidance. They want to escape from feelings of being trapped in their situation, and be empowered to make changes. With a few exceptions, no-one has to stay in an impossible situation - there is always a way out.

Doing this kind of work, you will find your clients complain about how hard it is to make changes. When you have heard these word many times, you will be able to remain calm and remind them that giving themselves negative messages is not helpful.

Once your client has accepted that only he can pull himself out of his dilemma, your work will move forward faster.

As he starts to think more positively, he begins to take on board your facilitation and make constructive suggestions of his own.

When you feel you have done everything you can to help your client, do not be afraid to tell him. If he is looking for easy solutions, either he will be shocked into making an effort himself or he will leave and try to find someone else to wave the magic wand.

Sometimes a client decides that what you have done to help him is sufficient for the time being. There may be deeper issues to be explored, but if your client does not wish to go into them he cannot be forced. He may well turn up again in the future when he feels strong enough to do some more work on himself. Some clients like to come every now and again for a 'top-up'. They are making the necessary changes in their lives, but still feel the need for some encouragement and reinforcement from you.

Clients who have reached such a stage of frustration that they will try anything, are often the most co-operative. They are usually willing to examine their childhood if necessary, even though it may be painful. Therapy can be very successful for such clients. They read the recommended books and do the homework. If their difficulties stem mainly from one or more 'forgotten' or half-remembered traumatic event, it may help them to bring back the memory. Hypnosis or visualisation techniques can be used to induce a trance state. You can then guide them through re-experiencing the event in order to see it differently. This alleviates the pain so that it no longer continues to affects their everyday life. Dramatic changes may occur very quickly. This is one of the most exciting and heartening aspects of being a therapist .

Couple Disharmony

Working with couples can be very rewarding. Progress is likely in the first session, when the couple experience talking to each other for the first time using a professional therapist as an intermediary. Much can be achieved by encouraging the couple to express their dissatisfactions to each other. By asking the kind of questions that make both parties listen carefully without jumping to conclusions, the therapist helps to highlight old patterns of behaviour. She is free to stop either partner in mid-flow and help them to see exactly what they are saying and doing, so that they become aware of their hidden agendas. Bringing these to the surface alone, gives a great sense of relief to the partners. Once they understand why some formerly inexplicable behaviour occurs, they no longer react to it in the same way. A common result of partner therapy is that one or both parties decide to have individual therapy to deal with their own issues.

Where both partners are willing to come for therapy the prognosis for the solution of the problems is good. If only one partner is willing to attend, you know that the other has a closed mind and is not willing to accept responsibility. In such cases the improvement in attitude of the client seeking therapy may result in the ending of the relationship.

Eating disorders

These complex disorders are best dealt with by experienced and specialist therapists, as in extreme cases, they are potentially life threatening. Most eating problems such as anorexia, bulimia or failure to eat regularly, have deep roots which go down to unconscious sources. Such cases are often extremely complicated and take a long time to explore, understand and treat. The nature of these unconscious sources is related to long-standing feelings of worthlessness, rejection and a desperate need for acceptance, leading even further down to an insecure and under-nourished childhood.

Long-term Clients

These are clients who require more than twenty therapy sessions. They need to be allowed to work at their own pace, as any attempt to hurry things along usually has the opposite effect. The therapist must take her lead from a client like this and continually strive to understand him, so that he senses she is gaining empathy with him. Once he begins to feel understood, his trust in her is strengthened and he is more likely to release those innermost secrets that he has never felt safe enough to reveal before.

Long-term clients are often vulnerable but at the same time quite determined to work through their difficulties. They usually have more than their fair share of symptoms, which accounts for their inability to find suitable work or relationship difficulties. Their childhoods are often full of traumatic events, some remembered, a few half-remembered and others so deeply submerged in their minds, that they have only the vaguest impressions of them. Hearing about these harrowing experiences makes you wonder how they managed to survive and grow up at all.

As in all therapeutic work, the strength of the relationship between client and therapist is the foundation on which progress is made. Without that special rapport nothing happens. You may recall how as a child you suddenly improved in a subject because you had a change of teacher, one you felt understood and liked you. It works the same way with client and therapist.

The therapy process can be described as a new and improved method of parenting. The client gradually learns to relate to his therapist as he needed (but failed) to relate to his real parents. She gently guides him through the maze of past misconceptions, unhelpful beliefs, negative thinking habits and the trail of nightmarish ghosts which emanate from old unresolved traumas. This helps him to face all those situations and people that have troubled him in his past, one by one.

As the work proceeds, the relationship between therapist and client changes. Initially, the therapist gives her client much-needed support and encouragement, and is careful to ensure that he goes away feeling better than when he arrived. She tries to keep him in a hopeful state of mind, dealing with negative attitudes as they arise and seizing any opportunity to allow him to see things more positively.

As her client gradually grows stronger and his confidence increases, the therapist begins to withdraw her support and interact more with him. He is now feeling confident and secure enough to be assertive and to challenge her. He dares to state when he is feeling impatient or when progress is too slow. He is approaching the rebellious phase all healthy teenagers pass through as they grow into adulthood. This accompanies the "transference", when the client no longer sees his therapist as the guru with all the answers, and treats her as though she had the same attitudes towards him as his parents and teachers.

At this point, the therapist is likely to feel annoyed when her client assumes she is judging him and becomes angry with her. After all, she is 'only trying to help'. These are the symptoms of 'counter-transference'. The client is beginning to touch on areas in which his therapist is not as confident as she would like to be. How she handles the situation is a test of her objectivity. She must not take her client's animosity personally, but see it as a sign that he feels comfortable enough to release painful feelings that have nothing to do with her.

The situation is resolved when the therapist's reaction to the transference is not what the client expects, because of his past experiences. With his therapist's help, he slowly begins to understand what he is doing, and his behaviour towards her gradually changes. This may happen quickly and is a just reward for the therapist's patience and refusal to let her own feelings deter her from her duty to her client.

Once the client has learned to handle his relationship with his therapist in a different way, this new skill is transferred to his other relationships in the outside world. He realises that it is his own actions and behaviour that cause him to be happy or miserable, fulfilled or frustrated. In other words, he knows he is responsible for his own life and no longer needs his therapist's help.

The therapist may find the ending of the work with her client painful, especially if she still feels she wants to be needed. However, if her main objective is to help her client take control of his own life, she will be more than satisfied at the conclusion of a successful piece of work. There are many other potential clients out there for her to help.

Again, the parallel with parenting is relevant. A good parent is pleased when his child feels confident enough to venture out alone. Parents who enjoy their work, whether professional, voluntary or recreational, have a sense of purpose and satisfaction that is not lessened by the end of any one phase of their lives.

Chapter Eleven

The first consultation

The most important consultation is the first. The initial impression you and the client make on each other is the decisive factor in how quickly rapport is established – and the sooner it happens the better. In this first session the therapist needs to work towards this aim. Then when the client departs at the end of the session, he feels confident in her ability to be of use to him, otherwise he won't come back.

Rapport

Rapport is a word you will hear repeatedly during therapy training. It refers to the special bond between client and therapist. Carl Rogers, the psychologist and founder of counselling, considered this relationship, known as the therapeutic alliance, to be of prime importance for a successful outcome to therapy. Indeed, most therapists believe good rapport is the most factor in the successful outcome of therapy. The essence of rapport is a sense of trust between two people. We all have certain hidden agendas which we should allow ourselves to acknowledge. A client needs to feel that he can talk about these without fear of being judged. When the therapist also has hidden agendas she is unaware of or cannot admit to, this may spoil the rapport with her client.

The following chart shows some typical examples of therapists' hidden agendas:

Agenda	Meaning	Harmful potential
I must be seen to be a good therapist	I must 'cure' my client	Therapist imposes her own theories on client and ignores client's own wishes
I'm afraid of making a mistake	My client won't trust me. My client will think I'm no good. I'll feel bad about myself	Client senses the therapist's unease, and consequently feels a lack of trust
I must make sure my client likes me	I'll feel hurt and undervalued if he doesn't like me	Client takes his cue from the therapist and fails to express his negative feelings. The therapist's lack of sincerity makes him feel uneasy
This client really annoys me	I wish I hadn't taken him on	Client senses this negativity and draws into his shell feeling angry
How much longer must I listen to this rubbish?	I know I should listen but I'm bored stiff	Client rambles on then gets angry with therapist for not helping him
I'm anxious the client should know I really care	I'm afraid my client will think I don't understand	Client senses the therapist's inner tension and clams up. Or he may start giving 'therapy' to encourage the therapist

■ *I must be seen to be a good therapist.*

If the therapist is thinking about the impression she is making, her focus is obviously not on her client. She should find out what her client's expectations are and come to a joint, mutually agreed conclusion on the aims of the work together. It is counter-productive to try to make a client do something against his will. If he does not want to get better, the therapist cannot force him to do so, nor should she wish to. Some clients terminate their therapy sessions when they discover they have to do some work themselves and that any change must come from them. In such cases, the client's decision must be respected.

■ *I am afraid of making a mistake.*

Anyone who is afraid of making a mistake will make a hopeless therapist. As in all aspects of life, it is sometimes necessary to take a calculated risk. Everyone is allowed some mistakes. If a therapist makes an error of judgement, she should own up to it. In all probability, the client will respect her honesty.

■ *I must make sure my client likes me.*

If you try to please, you will not succeed. You must be able to tolerate and deal with your client's negative feelings. The relationship engaged in is one of therapy not friendship. What is necessary is mutual respect.

Before starting to practise, all therapists should realise that they do not need other people to validate them. True self-respect means telling the truth as you see it. Therapists must be open with their clients, and this means pointing out to them behaviour and patterns they are probably unaware of. Although this is difficult, it provides material for exploration. As long as a therapist knows her client, has an intuitive sense of just how far she can go and is thinking only of his well-being, there is almost no limit to what she can say.

■ *This client really annoys me.*
It is not unnatural for a therapist to get annoyed with a client. As the guiding spirit, it is her responsibility to work out why she is so affected and to take action to change her attitude. Failure to do so will interfere with the work she is doing with her client.

■ *How much longer must I listen to this rubbish?*
A therapist does not have to listen; she chooses to listen because she wants to. When a client starts relating his catalogue of complaints, a therapist has every right to stop him and make it clear what he is doing by challenging his statements. This is quite appropriate and benefits both client and therapist. There are times to listen and times to intervene.

■ *I am anxious the client should know I really care.*
Don't worry about it. Stay relaxed and pay attention to the client's words and body language. This is enough to show you care.

Clients also have hidden agendas which the therapist must attempt to identify. She can then use her judgement when and how to communicate this information to the client. The following chart looks at some common examples of clients' hidden agendas, what they really mean and their potential harmful outcome:

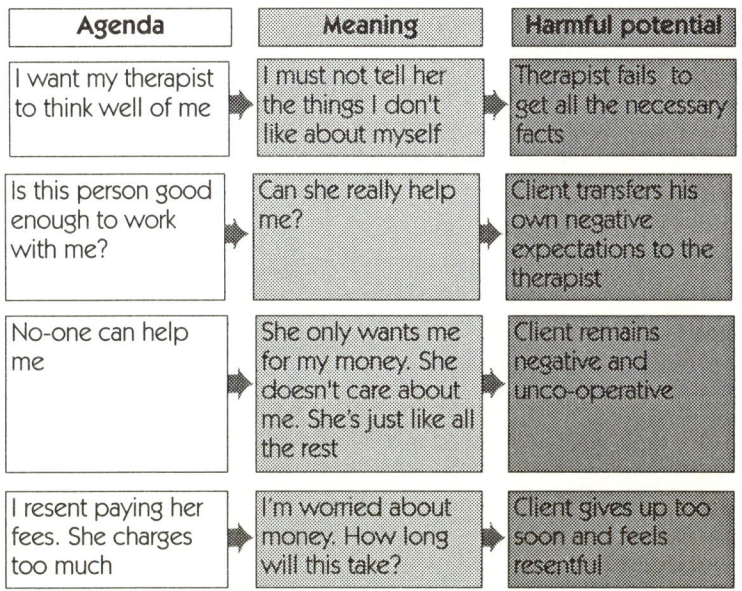

Agenda	Meaning	Harmful potential
I want my therapist to think well of me	I must not tell her the things I don't like about myself	Therapist fails to get all the necessary facts
Is this person good enough to work with me?	Can she really help me?	Client transfers his own negative expectations to the therapist
No-one can help me	She only wants me for my money. She doesn't care about me. She's just like all the rest	Client remains negative and unco-operative
I resent paying her fees. She charges too much	I'm worried about money. How long will this take?	Client gives up too soon and feels resentful

▓ *I want my therapist to think well of me.*

The desire to be well thought of is the most common hidden agenda. The therapist conveys her open-mindedness, tolerance and non-judgmental attitude by her behaviour and her speech. It usually takes more than one session to overcome this agenda. The client is probably used to other people being critical and has developed the habit of avoiding saying anything that is likely to annoy. A large part of all therapists' work is convincing clients to say whatever they like within the safe environment they have created.

▓ *Is this person good enough to work with me?*

The fear that the therapist is not good enough to work with is expressed in many different ways. The client may describe his dissatisfaction with former therapists, or he may enter with a faintly truculent attitude, as though daring the therapist to help him. She is an unknown quantity, so he is naturally apprehensive. This is not an easy agenda to deal with. One approach is to take firm control from the start while giving lots of support and reassurance. During the first session, congratulate him on taking the difficult step of seeking therapy, which shows he does believe he can be helped. Another approach is to help him see things differently by challenging his faulty thinking and upsetting his rigid beliefs.

■ *No-one can help me.*
A client who feels that no-one can help him has usually been to other therapists yet feels he has gained nothing. From his point of view, the next therapist is just another potential money waster. This is a tricky situation. Under no circumstances should the therapist try to justify herself, nor should she make promises she cannot keep. The client must realise that the results of therapy depend on his own efforts and that the therapist cannot do the work for him. He should be told that he is free to say whatever he likes and that his therapist is pleased when he questions her suggestions. She can point out that without his co-operation, nothing will be achieved. By playing devil's advocate, he is more likely to be convinced that she can help him.

■ *I resent paying her fees. She charges too much.*
Many people are willing to spend vast amounts on trivial items which may actually harm them, but are miserly when it comes to paying for their physical and mental wellbeing. Some people are genuinely hard-up and may be concerned that they are starting something they cannot afford to finish. The agenda about money is a sensitive one and is explored in a later chapter.

The initial greeting

What does the therapist do when she opens her door and is face to face with her first client? There is no one answer to what to do next. Some therapists think it is inappropriate to shake hands, others feel that the less the therapist says the better. The reasoning behind this is that the therapist should give as little away about herself as possible, especially in the early stages, to encourage her client to take the initiative. This is certainly true of psychoanalysis. Personally I think Carl Rogers' approach is the best – to be your natural self while at the same time focused on the client.

Everyone is unique so should be approached in a way that takes their individuality into account. Personally, I like to be spontaneous, finding my natural response is determined by my client's personality. If I open the door to a tiny lady who looks up at me like a frightened mouse, ready to run away at the slightest false move on my part, I would speak to her gently and take care not to invade her personal space. I would probably pass a few innocuous remarks about the weather to put her at her ease as she steps inside. My response to someone with a more outgoing nature would be completely different.

The therapist must be true to herself and only do and say what comes naturally to her. Clients quickly pick up on insincerity at an unconscious level. This makes them feel uneasy. Therapists do not need to have a special manner or a special voice. But they do need boundaries. These are dealt with in Chapter Sixteen.

The first session

The therapist should aim to establish a good rapport with her client as quickly as possible. She starts the first session gathering useful information in the form of a case history. If the client says "I don't know where to start," it can help to ask a few straightforward questions about age, marital status, number of children, occupation, and other details. All the time, a good therapist is paying attention to the client's body language, facial expressions and tone of voice. Sometimes it is possible to get straight to the heart of the problem by picking up on a grimace or miserable tone of voice in one of the responses. For instance, if the answer to the question "Is your mother still alive?" is "Yes" and is accompanied by a heavy sigh, this can be followed up with a few questions about the relationship with the mother. This is one way in.

Another route is for the therapist to ask directly: "Why do you feel you need to see me now?" Identifying the straw that broke the camel's back gives her important clues. She should listen carefully, especially to any mumbled, throwaway remarks at the end of sentences. This is when the unconscious mind is likely to break through with some vital piece of information.

Of course, the therapist can ask the obvious question: "What's your problem?" which may possibly uncover the real trouble. Sometimes there is no problem at all – the client is worrying about something that almost certainly will never happen. In such cases, one session may be all that is needed to make this clear to him. Cognitive therapy, which examines the role of language in underlying thoughts and attitudes, is very useful for dealing with this kind of situation.

People sometimes think they 'ought' to be worried and are living up to a role that others (they think) expect of them. In such cases, asking penetrating questions may be all that is necessary to enlighten them. However considerable skill is needed when questioning a client's statements or uncovering unhelpful beliefs and attitudes which are the actual cause of their distress. Once the problem is recognised, which may take several sessions to establish, the real work can begin.

Taking notes

Personally, I find note-taking during sessions invaluable. I keep my jottings as brief as possible, writing down anything that strikes me as being significant. The client's language patterns are important, and once these are picked up the therapist can make full use of them. It is an effective way of maintaining rapport.

Some therapists find taking notes distracts them from listening properly and also distracts the client, but I have not experienced this. As long as the rapport is good and the therapist keeps focused on her client there should be no problem, assuming she can think and write fast enough. Clients hate feeling they do not have their therapist's complete attention. (Remember your anger as a child, when you were trying to tell your mother something and her thoughts were elsewhere?)

If you find taking notes during a session difficult, you may prefer to write your comments at the end instead. When I am re-reading notes in preparation for a client's forthcoming visit, I find that a few phrases bring back whole tracts of a session that I might not otherwise remember. Much work may be covered in one session.

If a client comes to a session in a distressed state, the therapist's priority is to help him feel at least a little better before plying him with questions. She may need to allow him to release tears and verbalise his distress. Hypnosis and visualisation techniques are valuable tools in these situations, as they have a calming and relaxing effect and can be used before starting to identify the cause of the problem. The therapist must decide what is best for her client at that particular time and always try to send him away in a better state than when he arrived.

Ending the session

With some clients, the goals and aims of the therapy can be set during the first session. Sometimes, when the client fears being judged, the most important information does not surface immediately. The better the client knows and trusts his therapist, the more he lets go and gradually volunteers the information needed to help him. This is why listening is so important. If the therapist is not listening carefully enough, she may miss the mumbled remark at the end of a sentence that will give her the missing piece of the jig-saw puzzle. Always listen especially well when a client is about to leave. His imminent departure may mean he feels safe enough to say something really valuable. In my own practice, I finish a little early so that I can pick up on any parting remarks and work on them immediately in the last few minutes.

By the end of the first session, the client knows if he wants to come back and his therapist will have decided if she can work with him. If she feels that his case is beyond her skills, she may refer him to another therapist.

During the initial session, the therapist has set a good example by behaving openly and honestly. She has not made any promises she cannot keep, but at the same time has encouraged her client to feel hopeful. It can sometimes be difficult to get the balance right. She has also told her client that he is free to ask questions about the work and does not have to take anything on board he does not want.

During the first session it is important to lay down the conditions of work and the cost of the therapy. When these are clearly explained there can be no doubt in the client's mind about what happens if he fails to turn up for a consultation and when payment is due.

Chapter Twelve

The second consultation

The better a client feels after the first session, the higher his expectations for the second consultation. His therapist understandably wants him to retain these good feelings, especially if he has been considering therapy for a long time. The second consultation builds on and reinforces the work done in the first.

A common fear of many conscientious and caring therapists is that they will be unable to maintain the improved confidence of their client. Working with another person's problems is a challenging and complex task at anytime. The therapist should remember this and be as relaxed as possible about the work and avoid worrying about whether she is doing it 'right'. She can then concentrate on monitoring her client and responding to the covert messages he gives her. This allows her to be spontaneous and makes her role more effective.

Starting the session

A useful way to start any session is to ask the client how his week has been. Has he noticed any different feelings and, if so, what are they? Has he reacted differently to any everyday situations? Any open-ended questions which help him to remember without planting suggestions in his mind, are helpful.

Another way of starting the second session is to ask the client for his impressions of the first consultation and whether he has any questions about it. The client's feedback on the work is invaluable as it lets his therapist know what he found particularly useful. Therapists are often surprised that their client's recollections of what happened in a session are quite different from their own. This is of no consequence, as long as the session helped the client.

If a client becomes emotional immediately, hand him a box of tissues and allow him a little time to release his feelings. When this happens, he invariably apologises, so his therapist can validate him, by assuring him that she is pleased he feels comfortable enough with her to let go. Making use of any opportunity to show her client that she accepts whatever he offers without negative judgements or criticisms, cements the relationship. He will probably continue to apologise every time he releases strong emotions, and the therapist should continue to give him the go-ahead to do so. If it comes naturally, the therapist could use humour to reinforce her message. For example: "There you go again! I'm going to get you to put ten pence into this box every time you say sorry! I'll be rich in no time." When used sensitively, humour and laughter have powerful effects.

Continuing to collect information

At every session, the client will raise some issues he has not previously mentioned. Usually, the later these are revealed, the more important they are. These are his life's secrets, the things he is ashamed of and perhaps has never revealed to anyone else. They are the very things his therapist needs to know to help him. Sometimes the secrets revealed seem so trifling and unimportant to the therapist that she may find herself wanting to laugh in amazement. I once did this with a client: "Is that all?" I asked, as I nearly fell off my chair. My client couldn't believe her eyes – she gaped at me for a few seconds and then joined in the laughter herself.

Her symptoms had vanished by the time of her next appointment. This is an example of spontaneity, a deliberately conjured-up ploy would never have worked because the unconscious mind distinguishes between truth and fallacy. Therapists are frequently surprised by their clients, which is one reason why they should never jump to conclusions too quickly or think that they know best.

Information gathering can be speeded up by giving clients homework between sessions. The nature of this homework depends on the type of therapy used. For example, cognitive therapy has its own ideas on questionnaires and record-keeping, helping a client to notice how his feelings and thoughts change from day to day. Homework is also a test of a client's commitment to the work. It is worth point- ing out that by giving time and thought to his homework, the client will save money spent on therapy sessions as the work with the therapist will be completed sooner.

There are hundreds of self-help books available. Therapists should read as many of them as possible and decide which ones are particularly appropriate. I have found that recommending books to my clients is a great help to them and speeds up progress.

How long will it take?

Usually by the end of the second session, the therapist has a good idea of the severity of her client's difficulties and also of his temperament and character. The following points are the major factors affecting the rate of progress:

■ Childhood experiences form the basis of our beliefs and attitudes. A strong and naturally optimistic character can overcome much of the negativity of early, potentially damaging events. How we react to life's events depends on our inherited nature. What has a devastating effect on one person may be barely noticed by another. This is why children brought up in the same home in similar circumstances often react quite differently to life situations.

■ Sometimes a client's childhood has been one long history of emotional deprivation and abuse of one or more kinds. The lack of that loving care and facilitation provided by good parents and teachers, continues to affect even the hardiest character at a deep level in adulthood. Most of us bear some scars from the past. The person we are is the sum total of how we have dealt with our past experiences. Our character and personality determine how these experiences affect us.

■ Some therapists think it is unnecessary to delve into a client's past, believing that what matters is the present. Personally, I think that the present can only be understood by looking at the past. The study of history enables us to see past mistakes and how these can be avoided in the future. What applies to a nation also applies to an individual.

■ The question of how a person's future can be improved is answered by examining their reactions to early painful experiences. What did they do to survive them? How do they affect their present life? What can they do to exorcise old ghosts once and for all? We all have inner resources that we have developed unconsciously. A good therapist helps her client become aware of what these resources are, so that he can learn to use them again in the future.

Chapter Thirteen

Ongoing consultations
- the work begins to take shape

It is unusual for a client to leave after one or two sessions, but it happens. The client may have achieved his goal, or decided, when he realised what was involved, that he is not prepared to do the necessary work. It is also possible that he is not pursuing therapy because of the therapist. Perhaps she has been insensitive or too authoritative. One of my clients told me that he left one therapist after three sessions when she failed to remember the essential details of his case.

When a client returns for his third consultation it is because he has begun to see the value of the therapy and wants to continue.

What is the therapist really doing?
Therapy is creative work and after a while begins to take a shape of its own. The raw material is the nature of both the client and the therapist, plus the therapist's expertise. The nature of the client is at first the unknown quantity X. In order to help the client, the therapist first has to understand the function of X - how he works; what makes him tick; in other words, how he handles his life.

We have all learned ways of reacting to and dealing with everyday situations we encounter. These ways are called habits. When a person is faced with a new situation, he is thrown into a state of confusion. The television programme *Candid Camera* was immensely popular because it exploited this human peculiarity. The participants were unaware they were being filmed. These unsuspecting individuals were confronted with a totally unexpected event or behaviour, and the viewers enjoyed watching their responses. Most participants tried to ignore what was happening, because they were confused and could not believe their eyes.

When habits have been learned consciously, we are aware of each step. A good example of this is learning to drive a car. Once the individual moves have been mastered, they fuse together into one smooth action. We soon forget how we do this. It becomes automatic. Later on, if we try teaching someone else to drive, we have difficulty in breaking down this action into individual steps again. In the same way, we are not consciously aware of our unconscious habits.

Psychotherapists help their clients by firstly identifying learned habits that hold them back in life, and then break down the stages they go through when they perform the habit. Once this has been done, new moves can be learned to form a different, more helpful habit. The following case history illustrates this:

Jane

Jane visits her therapist with a problem. She feels awkward in company. She wants to learn how to talk easily with anyone, especially people she does not know. In these situations she blushes, and the more awkward she feels the more she blushes because she is terrified people will notice.

The therapist wants to find out how Jane learned this behaviour and how she has learned to blush to order. Blushing to order is an unusual skill, and when the therapist mentions this, Jane is confused. Why? Because she had always considered her blushing to be a disability, not a skill, like playing the piano.

The confusion frees Jane from her normal expectations. The therapist does not say: "How awful for you!" which is the response she expected to hear, so she cannot feel sorry for herself. (Pity for oneself or another plays no part in psychotherapy.)

The therapist then takes Jane step by step through what happens when she meets a group of people. Jane is not used to doing this. The therapist asks questions and patiently waits while Jane struggles to find the answers. The therapist leads her in slow motion from the moment she leaves home, through the journey to the venue, through her first impressions, to what she does when she gets there. Along this journey Jane is asked such questions as: "How are you feeling now? Where in your body is the feeling? Describe it. What are you seeing now? What pictures are you making in your imagination? Describe them. What are you hearing? What words are going on in your head?"

The journey takes time. Everyone makes pictures, hears voices, has feelings throughout the day, yet most people are quite unaware of this. Developing that awareness can be a slow process. The therapist must be very patient and give gentle encouragement.

After a while Jane responds to the therapist's questioning. Just before she enters the venue she says to herself: "I'm going to do it again. I know I'll start blushing when I feel eyes on me. I feel all agitated inside in my tummy and I've got a slight headache. I can see me making a fool of myself."

The therapist now has several important clues. Jane pre-programmes herself with negative instructions, such as: "I'm going to do it again." This is a very effective form of auto-hypnosis. Jane has control over her bodily functions, she knows (unconsciously) how to get her body to react to the negative suggestions, and this is why she is able to produce blushes so easily. Jane also has a poor self-image. She chooses to see herself in a bad light. She also believes that 'making a fool of yourself' is a bad thing. (The therapist could point out that comedians make a good living at it.)

Jane's therapist can now either work directly on the behaviour, or go deeper, uncover the underlying problem and help Jane to deal with it. In fact, she can do a bit of both. She has already realised that Jane suffers from the common complaint of low self-esteem.

Working at a deep level takes time and such a fundamental difficulty cannot be resolved in one session. In fact, Jane will probably continue working at valuing herself throughout her life. This does not mean she has to keep visiting her therapist – she can be taught the skills needed to acquire self-confidence. Once these are firmly in place she can do the rest for herself.

The therapist may work on the behavioural aspect. She may help Jane to acknowledge the confidence she already possesses by asking her to remember an occasion when she did something really well and was happy about the outcome. This can be something really simple, like cooking a meal. She is taken through the same steps in slow motion to help her remember pictures, voices and feelings. Then the therapist asks her to transfer the encouraging pictures, voices and feelings to the difficult situation. The therapist is transferring the same feeling of confidence Jane has already experienced in another situation, to the difficult one. These are neuro linguistic programming (NLP) techniques which are very useful.

Jane can choose whether to learn a few techniques to help her with her current difficulty or go for gold and work on the deeper issues. If she has enough determination she will decide to do the latter.

So Jane and her therapist embark on detective work, seeking out clues as to why and how Jane developed her lack of confidence and self-esteem. They need to look into her early family life and childhood events and find which significant events had the most detrimental effect. Jane will then be helped to perceive these in a different and more helpful way.

In the early stages of therapy Jane needs strong support. She has a lot of buried pain that must be brought to the surface and released. The therapist teaches her that it is acceptable to acknowledge her own feelings and not to make judgements about them. Jane says: "I know it's awful but..." over and over again until she begins to understand that it is safe to air any of her thoughts

Gradually, in this sheltered environment, Jane begins to stop saying "Sorry" so much and feels comfortable revealing more hidden aspects of herself. As the therapist unravels further clues, the underlying structure of Jane's inner nature begins to emerge, revealing how much of Jane's behaviour is innate and how much is learned. She begins to see the kind of person she is dealing with. The more a person's character has been distorted by the continual effort to fit in and to please others, the harder it is to find the real person behind the facade.

Inevitably, Jane has suffered at the hands of adults. If one or both of her parents inflicted the damage, this will create antagonistic feelings: she wants to believe that her parents really loved her and yet she is angry with them. The therapist's task is to allow Jane to express both sets of feelings. The hardest part is persuading Jane to acknowledge her anger and desire for revenge. She needs to understand that it is natural to feel resentment, but not helpful to act it out.

In my experience, however badly a child has been treated, he still wants to believe that his parents loved him. Feeling unloved strikes at the very root of our sense of self-worth, and is the reason so many abused children tend to idealise anyone who is the least bit kind to them. Abused children also find it hard to make balanced judgements about others and to acknowledge their good and bad points.

Jane's task is to accept her parents and/or teachers as they were and the fact that no-one is wholly bad or good. She needs to realise that while it is good to express anger against people who have ill-treated her, she must acknowledge that blame is not helpful. It is perfectly natural to want revenge, but to actually harm another person does not do any good. Jane needs a great deal of support to help her arrive at these conclusions.

Roles of the therapist

A psychotherapist or counsellor has many roles – a surrogate parent who allows her client/child to grow up and become independent; a teacher, showing her pupil how to deal with his life in new ways; and a detective, continually searching for clues and recognising underlying patterns.

The psychotherapist is also 'The Good Example', the one the client may not have had during his childhood. Although they are unaware of it, clients learn their attitudes and beliefs from their therapist. This is inevitable and cannot be helped. A therapist works through many of her own problems during training. The fewer hidden agendas she has the better. During therapy, her clients will learn much about her character, taking on board aspects of her personality that appeal to them and which they find helpful. A therapist, like a parent, leads by example.

Chapter Fourteen

The character of the therapist

The way that you work and how you use your skills is determined by your character, temperament and natural talents. If you try to copy someone else or stick too closely to the rules laid down by your own particular training, your work will suffer. A good therapist does the training, learns the rules, lets them sink into the unconscious, then has faith that the work will be done.

I believe that a genuine desire to help others is a calling, something a person is drawn to by a strong inner need to fulfil the meaning of life. Throughout my own life, I have felt this call, yet I tried other things first and used different skills. I learned a great deal and gained satisfaction. Yet, in the end, I was drawn into this work and find it the most rewarding I have ever done.

All kinds of very different people are therapists. To succeed you need certain natural talents and qualities of character. The talents include imagination, intuition, an ability to see patterns and make connections and an intense curiosity about human nature and the big questions of 'good' and 'evil'. The qualities of character required are common-sense, scepticism (so that you are not taken in too easily), determination and a love of challenges. You also need self-confidence and self-belief, open-mindedness, the capacity to admit to mistakes and to tolerate and work through frustrations. You also need lots of mental and physical stamina.

Whether you are introvert or extrovert is unimportant.

You may be voluble and love to talk or quiet and keep verbalisation to a minimum. All that matters is that you are a good listener.

Learning from other therapists

Most therapists are interested in learning about new techniques and approaches which can be introduced into their working methods when appropriate.

To this end, seminars and workshops are held every year so that therapists can see how some of the world's best practitioners work and learn from them. Although it is never a good idea to model oneself entirely on another person, these events are a useful way to enlarge your scope and flexibility.

I once attended a workshop with Dr Ernest Rossi, a close collaborator of Milton Erikson, a medical doctor who developed hypnosis in ways that had never occurred to anyone before. I had read Dr Rossi's books and been greatly impressed by them. I knew Milton Erikson was a flamboyant and forceful personality, so expected Ernest Rossi to be the same. To my surprise he was very different, almost the exact opposite. He was quiet, restrained, almost self-effacing, yet at the same time very much in control. I liked his gentle manner and the way he allowed his clients to be themselves.

Another interesting workshop was led by Dr Michael Yapko and Frank Farrelly. I had read Frank Farrelly's book *Provocative Therapy* and loved his approach. Acting as devil's advocate, Farrelly used his wonderful American/Irish sense of humour to make his client argue his own case instead of arguing it for him. The two-day workshop was therapeutic for all who attended. Farrelly takes risks by saying things to his clients that few therapists would dare, yet maintains tremendous rapport all the time.

I was so impressed that I tried using some of Farrelly's techniques with the first client I saw after the workshop. I made a hash of it and almost alienated my client for good. This experience reinforced my belief that when trying out new techniques or ways of working, we should always proceed with caution until we have digested what we have learned.

The other therapist, Michael Yapko, had a very thorough, reasoned approach to the treatment of depression. For many years Michael worked from a psychodynamic viewpoint. Now he believes in using Brief Therapy, which emphasises the need to concentrate on the present and future, by teaching clients new skills to make the changes they want. His seminar was so good that I took far more notes than usual and ordered three of his books.

All these therapists are exceptionally good at what they do and use very different ways of getting results. They have the confidence to be themselves and to do their work in their own particular way. The qualities they share are what all good therapists should aspire to, namely,

- the ability to make instant rapport;
- patience;
- a sense of humour;
- setting a direction without being overbearing or pompous;
- focusing on the client and constantly monitoring his body language and other signs;
- fluency in working and responding to the client's reactions;
- being able to change direction when necessary;
- being firmly in charge without being controlling or bullying.

Chapter Fifteen

The character of the client

Although every human being is unique, life experience shows that certain types of personality recur. After practising for a while, a therapist begins to recognise that there are also certain kinds of clients.

■ *The 'professional' client*

When a client has been to at least four other therapists and uses the phrase, "No-one has been able to help me", the therapist is probably up against someone who has made a career out of trying different therapies. It may seem odd, but there are people (fortunately few in number) who enjoy paying fees to prove they cannot be helped. This is an unconscious process as the client is unaware of the real motive. He seems to be boosting his ego by continually reinforcing his belief that his case is so difficult and unusual that no therapist is clever enough to help him. A therapist should not fall into the trap of trying to convince him that she is the exception, as she will find herself involved in a no-win situation. Every argument she puts forward will be triumphantly trounced. The harder she tries to convince him, the more he will enjoy giving her reasons why she cannot help him. A client like this is luring the therapist with flattery in the form of a challenge.

He should be made to do all the work. The therapist could try asking him: "What makes you think I can help you?" Or she can turn the tables and get him to argue his case as Frank Farrelly does. She should keep putting the ball back in his court which is likely to frustrate and annoy him because she isn't playing his game. With this type of approach, progress is made or the client leaves. Either way, the therapist avoids a no-win situation.

■ The guru-seeker

This client is usually full of enthusiasm at the start, with the hope that the therapist will turn out to be the 'expert' with all the answers that he has been searching for all his life. He must be disabused of this idea at once. It should be firmly explained that while his therapist is ready to help him discover the cause of his problems, he must do the work himself, including homework between sessions.

As the facilitator, it is not the therapist's place to tell him what to do, so she must be wary. This client wants to be dependent on someone else and it is only too easy to be inveigled into taking on that role.

I fell into this trap several times when I began to practise. One day, I realised the error of my ways when I asked my supervisor: "Why is it that the clients I work hardest with make the least progress while my successful clients don't wear me out at all?" She just looked at me and waited for the truth to dawn – and it did. If the therapist does too much work, her client will let her do so but fail to make progress. This particular client is trying to lure the therapist with a different form of flattery – by placing her on a pedestal. Remember that anyone on a pedestal can easily be knocked off.

■ Passive-aggressive clients

Repressed anger is the hidden agenda of this client, usually caused by unhelpful authoritive figures from their past. Their passivity means that they do not communicate well, because they are afraid of what they will say. This may seem like an unwillingness to co-operate, so you must be on your guard against becoming annoyed. You may even sense a certain hostility towards you. These clients feel angry at the very thought that they need help, but are unaware of this. Should you attempt to tell them this too soon, they retort angrily, "Of course I'm not angry!" and you will know your instincts are correct. (A strong negative reaction is usually a sign that one of the basic causes of their distress has been touched on.)

Fortunately these clients have their positive aspects. They have come to see you because they genuinely want to deal with their problem. They tend to have negative responses. so if you are getting monosyllabic answers or silence, it may be helpful to start talking yourself. Any subject will do. Try telling a story to help your client make connections and keep talking while you monitor their response. This may be a change in expression or a sudden physical movement. Then you can say "I see what I said has brought up something for you. Would you tell me what?" This rarely fails to produce a result and the answer is another clue to understanding them. I think it is a mistake to remain silent for long with someone like this. Silence can be quite threatening to a vulnerable person.

Establishing rapport with such a client is difficult, at least until they feel comfortable enough to release some of their inner anger. This may be directed against you, but is a good sign and not personal. You are merely the recipient of your client's anger towards the unhelpful people in his early life. Any kind of emotional response gives you useful material to work with and provides some of the most valuable clues. Such responses are probably more reliable than what the client tells you about himself. In this context, emotions don't lie. Reason can.

■ Losers and Victims

Some people habitually see themselves as victims. These are the clients whose hidden agenda is that you are one more person who is going to exploit them by taking money and not helping them. One source of their inner conflict is that at one level they do not expect to be helped, yet at another they do, or they would not have come to you. If permitted, they tell long tales of woe about all the things that have gone wrong in their lives. Do not allow them to do this because it only reinforces their negativity. Get to the bare bones of their past life by asking questions and stopping them from going into lengthy detail. Challenge the language they use. This serves the double purpose of breaking up their flow and making them see things differently. You will notice that losers use the passive tense constantly and take a negative point of view.

> *Client:* Well you see my mother made me leave school and I couldn't go to college.
>
> *Therapist:* Couldn't you have gone later as a mature student?
>
> *Client:* No I couldn't, I didn't have the money.
>
> *Therapist:* Perhaps you could have applied for a grant.
>
> *Client:* They wouldn't have given me one.
>
> *Therapist:* How do you know? Who are 'they'?
>
> *Client:* Nobody ever gives me anything I want.
>
> *Therapist:* What, nobody? Didn't your mother feed you when you were a child? How about trying to give yourself what you want?

And so on and so on. It is hard work. Your aim is to help this client to use his own resources so that he can help himself. If you persist, your client will begin to see that he is not absolutely powerless. Losers are dependent people. They expect things to drop into their laps so that they can give up trying and emotionally sponge on others. (There are plenty of people in the world only too willing to give support to victims.) Future counsellors, beware! You could easily become a victim yourself if your clients become too dependent on you. They may even ask you to reduce your fees because they cannot afford them. These people lose friends because they are too demanding. If they are ever to get any joy out of life, they must learn to accept responsibility for themselves and stop looking for props.

Not all losers lack money. Some are very successful at what they do, yet still feel they are missing out on the important things in life like good relationships. It is an attitude of mind. What they need is to change their basic belief systems and this can take months or even years to do.

■ Clients with a more positive attitude

Winners are not just people who are lucky, as is commonly believed. They are those who believe their fate is in their own hands.

Most clients seeking therapy or counselling are determined to change their lives for the better and most of them get what they want. These clients are winners. Whatever has happened to them in the past, they have some-how survived, kept their sense of humour and have a strong drive towards independence. They are willing to 'have a go' and co-operate, doing their best at homework and exercises.

■ Survivors of 'nervous breakdowns'

People who have come through a nervous breakdown are also winners. I dislike the term 'nervous breakdown'. It was used years ago, but today a more exact definition is 'reactive depression'. Like all labels, it is a loose way of describing many different states of mind when a person is unable to function properly. The symptoms of reactive depression are debilitating and include loss of interest and pleasure, feelings of worthlessness, impaired concentration and memory, emotional instability, too much or too little sleep and a variety of aches and pains.

I have worked with several people who were in the middle of a depressive state or just coming out of one. They have all been fighters. Most of them refused medication because they were afraid of becoming dependent on it. One discharged herself from a psychiatric hospital after two weeks against her doctor's advice, because it made her feel worse. Needless to say, this strong-minded young lady's refusal to accept what she didn't want, ensured that she made rapid progress in therapy. Let me add a caveat here. This lady was in no way psychotic. Had she been, a stay in hospital would probably have been essential. She was a high achiever who had suffered too much stress.

Such people appear to have managed well for years, building up careers and taking responsibility for themselves and others. People depend on them. They respond to that need by working too hard, until one day they collapse under the strain and realise they must make their own health their priority. One of their characteristics is persistence, which causes them to stay in a harmful situation for too long. One of my own clients stayed in teaching, believing that she would learn to cope with the stress. Had she realised earlier that teaching was not the right job for her, she might have avoided the breakdown situation by quitting earlier.

Many depressed or overstressed people belong to what we call the 'caring' professions. They have not learned their limits and have become ill from worry, the result of being too closely involved helping others. The nervous collapse acts as a warning to take stock of their own lives.

Excellent and effective therapy is possible in these cases because the client is particularly open to influence and strongly motivated to make changes. Progress can be astonishingly quick, although a true recovery requires understanding the underlying problem and resolving it. This usually takes some time, maybe six months, maybe a year or more.

Of course not all nervous breakdowns follow this pattern. Breakdowns sometimes occur when a client loses the person they have been dependent on. You will soon recognise the difference. The negative client blames everyone except himself - fate, lack of help from others, unfeeling children, and so on. Their favourite phrases are "It's not fair" and "Why should this happen to me?" to which the only possible response is "Why not? Someone has to be in the plane crash, someone has to win the lottery."

■ The Client who is misinterpreting the facts and wants to understand why she feels confused

One way of recognising confused winner types, is by the amount of energy they bring with them.

One of my own clients came in like a cyclone. It was only with the greatest difficulty that I managed to speak at all during the first part of the session. The amount of pent-up frustration was phenomenal. Depressed people never behave like this. Finally, I had to take a firm line and ask her to stop talking. I explained that if I could not intervene, she would derive no benefit from the session, apart from releasing her feelings. We then worked for over an hour, and I interrupted her constantly to question her assumptions. During this time, she made one connection after another, acknowledging each revelation with a thunderstruck expression and a few moments of welcome silence.

I have never seen anyone change their point of view so quickly. She departed feeling happy and relaxed after a brief session of hypnosis, astounded that she had not seen the truth for herself before. No sooner was she home, than she phoned, saying how much better she felt and could she come again the next day for another double-session.

She spent the weekend with her daughter, (who was amazed at her different attitude) and had already started making the necessary changes by her next appointment.

You might well ask, if she recovered so quickly, why could she not have done the work by herself? Why indeed! The simple reason is that we all have our blind spots and need someone else to show us what they are. This particular lady had always behaved according to a code of behaviour learned in childhood. Despite the fact that she was a strong and capable person, she had never been through a rebellious phase in her life. We need to experience this to decide what is right for us and how to avoid being influenced too much by other people's beliefs. Once my client understood this, she changed her beliefs in a few days. She then realised that what she had thought of as a great misfortune, was in fact a lucky break. Her whole perception of life changed.

▨ The Client who has never been listened to

For some people the best thing about therapy is having the undivided attention of another person, perhaps for the first time in their lives.

One of my clients described his sessions as his weekly treat, his indulgence. It rapidly became clear that he did not think he had a problem. He liked the way he was and was prepared to put up with the disadvantages of some of his behaviour because it also brought him rewards. It was several weeks before I fully realised this.

What he needed most was to feel validated by a person he could trust. I was still trying to understand his 'problem' and, finding myself unable to clarify it, I asked him what he wanted. How could I help him?

We had already worked on the reason he had come initially – a certain difficulty with someone he worked with. This had been resolved when he was offered a better job which removed him from the situation causing the problem. We also identified that he let other people control him too easily, yet he did not seem to mind this, as long as he liked the person. I was confused. What did he really want? Simple. He wanted someone to listen to him, to give him encouraging feedback and reassure him that he was fine the way he was. He said he needed to talk with me for a time and would let me know when he had had enough. We enjoyed several more pleasant sessions until he reached that point. It was the easiest work I have ever done.

The nature of the client determines your approach. He arrives with certain hopes and expectations which may change once the work starts. For this reason, it is a good idea to keep a close watch on the progress made, as it is easy to lose touch with the original purpose of the therapy.

A list of the client's expectations and the aims of the work should be made during the first consultation. At a later stage, if you feel you have lost direction, ask your client if he feels he is making progress. His answer will enable you both to take stock of what has been achieved and the work still to be done. Assuming that you have written clear notes, it is a chance to remind him of his initial difficulties so he is aware of what he has changed. Clients often overlook the progress they have made because they are focused on what they still have to do. It is encouraging for them to look back down the road and realise just how far they have come.

The therapist's aim is not to impose, but to take the raw material offered. By helping her client make something of it, he will enjoy greater satisfaction in life, a stronger sense of his own identity and the confidence to follow his own natural inclinations. As long as society's wellbeing is not compromised (if he wants to rob a bank he must understand that such action is not appropriate), the result is a happier, more fulfilled life.

Chapter Sixteen

Winners and losers

- *what is living for?*

Winners are usually thought of as people who achieve worldly success, fame and fortune. However, in this book, I use the word to describe people who lead fulfilling lives, knowing that they are using their talents to make some beneficial contribution to the world. By contrast, losers are usually disillusioned people who die in a discontented and bitter state of mind, regardless of their position in society.

It is not what happens to you but how you respond that determines your life. On the whole we make our own luck. Of course it is possible to be in the wrong place at the wrong time and experience a plane crash, earthquake or the trauma of being caught up in a war through no fault of your own. However, we cannot attribute all the negative things that happen to us to bad luck. This would be refusing to accept responsibility for bringing things on ourselves, because we failed to think ahead and take action.

Thinking long-term
Businesses often fail because they do not recognise the difference between 'urgent' and 'important'. The same applies to individuals. Urgent matters are those that would cause us immediate problems if not dealt with by a certain time – returning income tax forms and paying our telephone bill fall into this category. We pay a penalty if we fail to do

urgent tasks (we get fined or the phone is cut off), so most people do them, albeit reluctantly. These are short-term problems.

The more important things of life are usually long-term and involve thinking ahead when it is not immediately necessary to do so. If we delay this essential planning, we create difficulties for ourselves in the future.

Priorities

Doing what is right for us is more important than pleasing other people. Prioritising is important for business organisations too, because our personal wellbeing is closely related to society as a whole. The neuroses holding back individuals are the same ones preventing social progress.

To know what your priorities are you have to consider your life in the long-term. Living from day to day without thinking about where it is leading, is a recipe for disaster, yet is a pattern many of us follow. It is a major cause of the uncomfortable symptoms and lack of ease that causes people to seek professional help.

To become a happier and more fulfilled person, a client is encouraged to look at his life as a whole. With his therapist's help, priorities can be set to help him achieve his goals.

Sometimes the thought of making life changes that are likely to alienate other people creates a real fear of isolation and loneliness. We may be frightened that we will not be liked, or will not 'fit in'. We may have become so used to our own distorted behaviour (our way of 'getting on' with others) that we have lost touch with our needs.

Thinking about what is good for us gradually makes us more content. If we are always trying to please others by 'fitting in', we invariably end up full of hidden resentment and anger. These feelings surface when we are tired or under extra pressure, so that our inner irritation becomes obvious to those around us. This sours our interactions and defeats the aim of the exercise, which is to be accepted, creating a vicious circle.

All frightened and unhappy people affect those they come into contact with as well as themselves. People who have lived their lives 'doing their duty', often feel frustrated and bitter as they get older. They cannot understand why their 'good' behaviour has not been rewarded. The facts are that we make our own rewards by ensuring that we spend our time doing work that suits us and making friendships that nourish us.

Losers, Life-destroyers

■ Controllers

There are two kinds of controller. The first is a person who puts the desire to please others at all times before honesty and his own wellbeing. Such people initially overwhelm you with their charm, but gradually make you feel uneasy in their presence because you are not dealing with the real person. You are face to face with a mask. You sense the underlying lack of sincerity and feel worse after spending time with them. This is the more subtle kind of control.

The second type of controller has a compulsive need always to be right. All dictators, benevolent or otherwise come into this category. When taken to the worst extreme, the result of this attitude is imprisonment, torture and death, as the dictator tries and fails to convert others to his point of view.

Why do people want to control the lives of others? Is it not obvious that we are all different and that it is hard to know what is best for ourselves, let alone for others? Yes indeed, but human nature is such that sometimes the most obvious things are too close for us to see.

We want to control others when our own lives seem out of our control. Everyone does it to some extent. The most obvious example is when we encourage our children to do well in all subjects at school instead of letting them concentrate on topics they like. We do this because we feel they need as much education as possible to do the more interesting and higher paid work in the world, and because we feel we have a duty to do our best for our children. These are worthy aims undoubtedly and it is true that all children need guidance. However, we also need to respect our children's special gifts and ambitions.

A therapist has a responsibility to her client to avoid changing his life for him. Of course, she should be in control of the work and have a direction, but must avoid the temptation to override her client's right to choose what he wants to do. At times this requires great discipline on her part. It is so tempting to do the client's work, especially when they cannot see what is so obvious to the therapist. This is why patience and a good sense of timing are essential qualities in a professional therapist.

■ Bigots, Victims and Martyrs

The bigot and the victim are the opposite sides of the same coin. The first believes he is always right, the second that he is always wrong. Both attitudes have a depressing effect on others. Both make excessive demands on the therapist if she lets them. They exercise control in different ways - the bigot tries to convert you to his way of thinking, the victim makes you feel sorry for him and drains your time and energy.

Martyrs are a type of victim. They wear themselves out trying to be of use to others. They never rest and make other people feel guilty by continuing to work when everyone else is taking a break. They usually have a worried expression and complain frequently about how tired they are. This type of behaviour may be caused by having a parent or teacher whom they could never satisfy. Nothing they did was ever good enough, so they go through adult life trying to live up to an impossible goal of perfection.

You are not likely to encounter a bigot in your consulting-room, but will certainly meet your share of victims and martyrs. They are not easy to work with and will be the most demanding of your clients. However, they can be helped to change their attitudes by learning to judge themselves less harshly. Occasionally a loser can be helped to see himself as a winner. If you succeed in doing this you will feel a well-deserved sense of achievement.

Winners, Life-enhancers

■ Being a 'good example'-

If you are a winner yourself and want to help others, then you are bound to be successful. You are helping others for all the right reasons, not because you want to sort yourself out. You know how to encourage without overdoing it and have no hidden agenda because you are satisfied with your own life. You will be that wonderful life-enhancing influence, a good example. Like everyone else, you have moments of doubt and feelings of self-pity, but have learned the art of using doubt to exercise caution, and of rescuing yourself from the victim position.

The more you resolve your inner conflicts and achieve harmony in your life, the more you will be in touch with your own talents and creativity. Nothing is more rewarding or gives a greater sense of your own identity and self-worth than achieving something through your own efforts. The more you work on the raw material of yourself, the less you need other people's approval. Relationships become more enjoyable because you are not dependent on them. This helps you and your clients, who benefit from the lessons they unconsciously assimilate from being in your presence. You have become a life-enhancer yourself. Being a good example is a bonus for your clients.

Chapter Seventeen

Supervision

- *ongoing review of work*
- *objectivity and subjectivity*
- *transference*
- *boundaries*

Supervision

Difficulties inevitably arise whether you have been practising one month or five years. This is why supervision is necessary. Supervision is a formal arrangement whereby therapists can regularly discuss their work with an experienced psychotherapist or counsellor. Most institutions giving accreditation make regular supervision a requirement for membership. and can recommend someone suitable in your area. However good we are, we all have blind spots and need someone we respect to help us see them. Respect is essential, so choose your supervisor with care. If you later feel you are not comfortable with her, choose someone else. Everyone needs freedom of choice.

Your supervisor should monitor how she works with you, just as you monitor your own work with your clients. You may find yourself getting angry with her, in the same way your clients get angry when you uncover their sensitive and unacknowledged hidden agendas. When this happens, you know you have a good supervisor. Her brief is to listen to the difficulties you encounter and help you to find new ways of tackling these problems. By being conscious of what is happening to your client (and to yourself), you become more aware of how you work and of finding ways to improve your own methods.

Objectivity and Subjectivity

Whatever anyone says, it is impossible to be completely objective. If you accept this as a fact, you are less likely to allow your subjectivity to intrude inappropriately on your work. You can only develop this kind of awareness by ongoing personal development. The best way to do this is to undergo the therapeutic process yourself with a therapist you respect. We all have our blind spots and another person can help us acknowledge and come to terms with them. Having the courage to face ourselves and delve into the deepest recesses of our minds shows that we have the strength to do the same for others. The kind of people we are affects our work and personal style. The more willing we are to challenge accepted ideas and the influences surrounding us, the more capable we are of coming to our own conclusions, developing an individual style, trying out new ideas and taking calculated risks with our clients.

I mentioned before that it is a great mistake to feel sorry for your clients. You may have this unhelpful tendency if you are too keen on 'helping' others. The process of therapy is not a case of the strong helping the weak. When someone has decided to use their hard-earned money to try and resolve long-standing difficulties, you can assume that that person has enough strength to do the work. They want to be shown how to do it themselves, and with your help, will quickly realise that they must play an active role in the work. Accept them as clients if you feel sufficiently confident that they will take responsibility for themselves and that you can deal with their particular problems. Remember, your beliefs and attitudes affect your client, as do the clothes you wear, your manner and body language, your tone of voice, verbal mannerisms and vocabulary. You are not just a blank screen on which your client projects his own nature, as some psychoanalysts have believed in the past.

Transference and counter-transference

Whatever you do, your client will project his interpretation onto you, based on his own attitudes and beliefs. This process is called 'transference'. It happens every day in all situations and sometimes masquerades as mind reading or intuition. Paranoid people transfer their hidden aggression (of which they are desperately afraid) to others, making their encounters appear threatening. A controlling person transfers his unacknowledged desire to have power over others, when he thinks others are trying to control him.

As a therapist, it is essential that you understand this process. We may pride ourselves on our intuition, and it is certainly a valuable asset, but always test any intuitive conclusions you reach. Intuition is coloured by personal experiences and beliefs, and you may be wrong. The difference between each and every one of us is enormous. Never assume you know everything about someone. You do not.

If you gain a reasonable understanding of yourself and your own unconscious processes, you will be ahead in your understanding of how human nature works. This is why therapists should experience the same therapeutic process as their clients – ongoing work on your own personal development is of the greatest importance. The more we know about ourselves, the better we handle counter-transference – our instinctive response to a client's behaviour towards us. When a client begins to vent his repressed anger against us for something which is not our responsibility, we must be able to handle the situation and control our natural inclination to fight back. We must avoid reacting and do something different.

Boundaries

It is essential to be true to yourself in the capacity of therapist. Your client is not in a relationship with you as a close friend. Yet your client must be convinced that you are concerned about them. Your approach is strictly professional as well as friendly. It is an intimate relationship, entirely different from any other kind.

Because of your profession, you can ask searching, personal questions which you would not dream of asking a close friend. Whilst taking care not to upset a client gratuitously, the caution and tact exerted in the outside world is not appropriate here. If you are doing your work well, your client will not always like you. You must receive his anger, frustration, impatience and other buried emotions without taking them personally. You are glad your client feels safe enough to talk about his innermost feelings that he has the greatest difficulty expressing in the outside world. You acknowledge that you are pleased this is possible and assure him that you understand. This is such a different response to what he is used to, that his feelings of frustration and helplessness change into a state of confusion, leading to new understandings.

It is not wise to become socially friendly with clients undergoing therapy. The boundaries may become blurred. Your behaviour with a client in a pub cannot be the same as in the consulting room. Some people assume you are on duty the whole time. "Are you analysing me?" is a question I am often asked at social functions. "No," I reply, "Not unless you're paying me."

'Doing therapy' effectively is hard work and requires great powers of concentration. If you take your attention away from your client for a few seconds, you may miss a vital piece of information. With friends you can relax and be yourself, but when that friend is also your client, the situation is more difficult. If you want a client to become a friend, it is best to move on to this relationship after the therapy is finished. If the client needs more work with you later, always undertake it in the formal setting of your consulting room and treat it as a professional consultation.

Money

This is an area which often causes problems. Your fees and how they are to be paid must be made clear to all clients before you start working with them. Always try to collect fees at the time of the consultation, as it obviates waiting for your money and sending out bills. Beware of people who 'forget their cheque books' at the first consultation. Obviously, a regular client who occasionally forgets is a different matter. Such a situation can be examined during the session, and any hidden agendas explored.

Once, a client who had been with me for over a year arrived without any money. This was so unusual that we spent ten minutes finding out why this had happened. It transpired that he was feeling annoyed that he was not making enough progress and was resentful about 'wasting' his money with me. This was the first time he had ever mentioned dissatisfaction. He was usually so passive and would never have had the courage to tell me directly how he was feeling. Needless to say, this was the beginning of a marked increase in his assertiveness. He was pleased about that and there were no further problems about paying.

If someone asks you to reduce your fees, consider it carefully before agreeing. Paying the full amount is a measure of the client's commitment to the work. People who pay for a service requiring their participation, work harder because they want value for money. When I was in training and gave my services free, I found that clients were far less conscientious about turning up on time and doing homework. It seems that we value something more when we have to pay for it.

I occasionally reduce my fees if I am working for research purposes, or if a client is in financial difficulties and I want to continue working with that client because it is useful to me. Some people ask for reductions as a matter of course, not because they cannot afford the fees. Most people who are serious about therapy do not ask for a reduction. Remember, your work is your livelihood and you are not a charity. Nevertheless, the decision is yours. You must decide for yourself, bearing in mind the caveats given.

If you have any doubts about boundaries, consult your supervisor. She will probably advise you to devise your own. It is easy to get drawn too far into a client's problems and do more for them than the conditions of the work demand. This is not good for either of you. You may become resentful if a client is demanding and you are doing too much of the work. If you allow yourself to be manipulated into such a situation, you may well lose something vital – your client's respect.

Chapter Eighteen

When therapy finishes

The time comes when you have done all you can for your client. Either you or your client will arrive at this conclusion, after which you have to make a joint decision.

Negative aspects of finishing

Your client may simply not come back. If that happens, you can either do nothing or try to contact him by phone or letter to discover the reason.

If the client fails to turn up for a session, you could phone him in case he has mistaken the date or perhaps forgotten his appointment. Your client may feel awkward about telling you he wants to stop having therapy. If he has 'forgotten' the session and makes another appointment, you can explore the reason for his forgetfulness. It may prove enlightening; perhaps he feels he is not making progress. You then have something to work on.

When you cannot contact your client because he fails to reply to your letter or return your message on the answer-phone, you know he does not want to return but is afraid to tell you directly. In such cases it is best to do nothing more. Trying to persuade a reluctant client that he needs to continue is counter-productive.

On the rare occasion that this has happened to me, I already had an inkling that the client had had enough. If I sense this feeling coming on, I always inform my client at once. Sometimes he insists that he still wants to continue because he feels he is benefiting from the therapy. After we have examined what he thinks he has gained from our consultations, some new information may emerge which helps me to see the way forward.

If the situation is still stalemate, I usually suggest a break of a few weeks, after which he can take up the work again if he wishes. This often makes a difference. The time without you can be valuable for him. and if he does decide to come back at a later date, you will notice changes in his attitude. The strongly motivated client who returns is more likely to succeed than the one who comes back reluctantly.

Chapter Nineteen

Conclusion

Coming to the end of a book is like finishing work with a client. Have I given my client what he came for? Is he leaving with increased insight and an awareness of his real feelings and needs? Does he think more clearly? Has he acquired greater objectivity? Have I done the job I set out to do?

You are presumably reading this book because the idea of becoming a counsellor or psychotherapist appeals, although you have no idea what it is like to actually do the work. I hope that the facilitation I have attempted to give has been helpful and that you have gained some insight into whether this work is something you still want to do. I have tried to give you a balanced picture of what it is like to be a therapist and shown you some of the pleasures and the difficulties involved.

This book has evolved from my notes made over the years and from my life events and professional experience of working with clients. Many of the topics covered in these pages could easily be expanded, but time and space are limited and choices had to be made. I have deliberately reinforced some of the most important points by repeating them with fresh emphasis in different chapters.

The bibliography includes books that have influenced my own work and others that I recommend to would-be counsellors and therapists. I know that reading the great writers of the literary world contributes as much to understanding the human psyche as wading through huge quantities of works about psychology and philosophy.

To be a successful counsellor or therapist, you need logic, intuition, imagination and an unremitting ability to hunt for clues. I regard psychotherapy as an art form, rather than a science.

I could not work without believing that there is a power greater than ourselves, although I do not know what that power is and do not accept any one religion. Like the eminent psychotherapist Jung at the end of his life, I believe a benevolent power exists but do not know how or why. I do know that it is essential for all human beings to feel useful and that life is meaningful and has a purpose that transcends the struggle for survival. So much of our disaffection in life stems from the lack of such a purpose, regardless of the difficulties we may have to contend with.

Many people come into therapy looking for happiness. But happiness is not a goal. It is an elusive feeling that happens unexpectedly when we use our particular talents to give pleasure and enjoyment to ourselves and to others. Developing our individual potential and the contribution this inevitably makes to our relationships and the world around us, is what gives us most satisfaction.

Chapter Twenty

Two case histories

I have stressed throughout this book that therapists do not 'cure' clients. Clients cure themselves by getting in touch with their own healing resources. To work successfully, therapists need training, daring and intuition so they know which skills to use, when and with whom. Sometimes, however much we want to help, we are unable to do so. This is because clients find their motivation to change is not strong enough, or they are not ready, or because we cannot find a way through with a particular client. Sometimes, when both therapist and client are patient enough, what looks like an insurmountable problem, can be gradually resolved over a long period of time.

Occasionally, I have had the experience of working with a client who makes a spectacular improvement very quickly. Here are two recent examples.

Caroline

Caroline is a young mother, in her late twenties, with two young sons, aged one and three years. The births had been particularly difficult and both children had been beset by minor health problems ever since. Caroline has a kind and understanding husband – an important factor for our work together. Therapy is far more likely to succeed when there is support at home.

Caroline arrived for her first session. She looked tired, not having had a good night's rest for a long time because both her children had a pattern of fitful sleeping and frequent awakenings at night caused by their health problems. Caroline herself, was suffering from irritable bowel syndrome (IBS) and also had psoriasis over most parts of her body, and particularly on her arms. Her doctor had pre-scribed a medicated cream to apply to the skin which had not made much difference. The same day Caroline began work with me, she embarked on an exclusion diet, to discover if she was allergic to certain foods.

Despite all the worry and stress of the previous three years, my first impressions of Caroline were of someone optimistic and positive. It was interesting that the onset of IBS coincided with the birth of her first child. Four years previously, I had attended a course using hypnosis for the treatment of IBS. Although I have since treated only two clients with this problem, both made a great improvement.

I decided that hypnosis could be helpful for both ailments. First of all, I needed to know Caroline's history so I could search for clues to any other aggravating factors in her life. Caroline had had an unsettled childhood and, like many children, had been negatively criticised and rarely praised. She had grown up feeling that she must work hard to please others.

A particular aunt, who had been one of her carers in child-hood, was in the habit of constantly ringing up to complain about the emptiness of her life. Being a kind person, Caroline had put herself out to do things for her aunt, yet nothing seemed to please her.

I pointed out to Caroline that she had enough to do with caring for her own family, and that her aunt, who is in good health, needed to be encouraged to take care of herself and to be less demanding. This was something Caroline had found very hard, although she admitted feeling fed up and resentful about giving up her valuable time when it did not seem to do any good. The difficulty kind people have in saying 'no' to those who make unreasonable demands on them is a common occurrence. When it is suggested that they resist these demands, they usually respond with "yes, but" – "Yes, but I love my father/ mother/sister/brother, so I must help them." In Caroline's case, all she needed was a ittle encouragement as she had already reached the point of knowing she must make a stand.

When I gave Caroline an initial test for her ability to go into a trance state, I was amazed at the promptness of her response. I realised that she was exceptionally suggestible and therefore very likely to respond well to hypnosis. This indeed proved to be the case. I recorded my voice so Caroline could take a tape home. A tape recorded during a session greatly reinforces the power of the suggestions.)

I use hypnosis *after* working with the client, so I am focused on what particular kind of suggestions will be most useful to them. I can then let my words flow spontaneously. For Caroline, we agreed that her most immediate need was to relieve tension in order to induce relaxation. My words centred on her need to take care of herself, to be comfortable with saying "no" when that was appropriate, and to get in touch with her healing processes. I stressed the fact that Caroline had far more power over her own body than she realised.

Caroline greatly enjoyed her first experience of hypnosis and went away looking quite refreshed. It is amazing how different people look after a session of hypnosis. Caroline's facial expression, especially her eyes, reflected calm and wellbeing. She returned the following week looking much less tired. The psoriasis on her arms was improved and her IBS symptoms had lessened. She had listened to the tape during the day, when the children were resting and found herself dropping off to sleep. Occasionally she used the tape twice a day, and managed two cat-naps, which helped her cope better with the disturbed nights.

During the week, her aunt had phoned as usual, and Caroline had said "no" to her demands without too much difficulty and without feeling guilty afterwards.

She had decided to take more exercise and had gone swimming twice in the week. She told me she had heard a talk on the radio about cranial-sacral therapy and how useful it was for children. She asked if I knew of anyone doing this work,. so I gave her the name of a colleague. Caroline took her small son to see her and he began to improve, becoming less easily upset and calmer after just one session. This was another factor helping to set Caroline's mind at rest.

Caroline continued to make rapid improvement and was completely free from all her physical symptoms after only four consultations – an astonishingly quick recovery. She accepted my advice that she must put her own wellbeing first, as everyone she loved would benefit and become more assertive and less prone to being manipulated. She also gave up the exclusion diet and ate normally after her last session with me.

When I phoned to check on her progress, she told me she was still completely free of all symptoms and both she and her husband were delighted with the results.

Mark

Mark is thirty-nine years old and travels all over the world for his company. He enjoys his work even though it is stressful (always the way with people in high-powered jobs). A certain amount of stress is exhilarating and necessary for us to maintain our physical and mental agility. As NLP tells us, it is not what happens to us that matters, but how we respond to situations and deal with them. Some individuals have strategies which enable them to tolerate a high degree of stress which would make other people ill.

When Mark was seventeen, he started having spells of sickness and numbness with headaches. He checked these symptoms in medical books and concluded he was suffering from migraine. Over the years, these attacks gradually occurred more frequently. Two years ago, he was having an attack every two or three months. The incidence of the attacks continued to increase until he was suffering one a week. This coincided with an improvement in his career and the need to travel more often. As his condition worsened, he sought medical help and was prescribed medication, but even this did not stop the attacks. He followed medical advice and removed chocolate, dairy products and eggs from his diet while reducing his alcohol intake to a moderate level. But still the attacks persisted.

Looking at Mark's history, there was no evidence of any unresolved trauma that could be a precipitating factor. His father died when he was ten. He had been on good terms with his mother and seemed to have worked through the bereavement in a healthy way. When he was thirteen, he knew a boy who suffered from migraine and often had to have time off school. At that time, Mark had a strong dislike of school and it seemed that feigning headaches would be a good way of staying at home. Although this was only a passing thought, Mark remembered the incident well (always a sign that it might be important). As I quickly realised how suggestible Mark was, it seemed possible that the idea of using migraine as a defensive strategy might have taken root in his unconscious mind.

Migraine is a painful experience and the more frequent

the attacks, the more obsessed Mark had become with anticipatory fears. He would wake every morning thinking, "Will this happen to me, today?" Such thoughts and their persistence cause great anxiety and may actually increase the likelihood of the onset of what is feared (sometimes described as a self-fulfilling prophecy). The more Mark's mind was preoccupied with fearful apprehension, the more his concentration wandered and he had difficulty getting down to his work.

As I listened to what Mark was saying, I noticed that he was very imaginative, open to suggestion and found it easy to describe his inner feelings and thoughts. This indicated that some NLP exercises combined with hypnosis might be the most appropriate treatment for him. This proved to be the case.

One of the first distressing signs of Mark's migraine was flashing lights behind his eyes, accompanied by a pulling sensation. We did some visualisation exercises where he remembered what these lights were like and defined them through their colour, shape and light intensity. He then projected this vision outside his head and I asked him to change his perception of the lights, making them darker and lighter, dimmer and brighter, larger and smaller, nearer and farther. Some people have great difficulty doing this kind of exercise, but Mark was exceptionally good at it. He was amazed at how easily he could bring back the sensation of the lights and change his perception of them.

Encouraged, we embarked on a second exercise. This was to help him eliminate or at least diminish the negative questions he was continually asking himself, such as "Will I be alright? Might I get a migraine today?"

Mark's frequent travelling made his situation worse, as he feared becoming ill in a strange place and being unable to go home and rest. I encouraged him to use his imaginative powers to remember how he felt when he first woke up in the morning. We then checked what pictures he was making in his head, exactly what he was saying to himself and how this affected his bodily feelings and emotions. I asked him to recall a time in his life when he was carefree and coping well, and asked him to remember the pictures, words and feelings associated with such memories. I helped him to relate these positive images with waking up in the morning, making them very strong and powerful, so that the negative images were eliminated.

Again, Mark responded well. In fact, by the end of the session, I noticed that he was gazing fixedly at the wall, already in a trance state. It was easy to start talking and help him become more comfortable, deepening the trance. My words reinforced everything he had learned to do. I suggested that he taught himself to change his perception of time. If he lived fully in the present he could concentrate on the job in hand and feel a greater sense of ease, leaving the future to take care of itself. I gave him a tape to take away and play every day.

Mark was impressed at how different he felt after this first session. He departed in a quiet, reflective state of mind. When he returned the following week, he reported that he had felt very relaxed and quite different after our session. Unfortunately, after a few days he suffered a severe migraine attack. He took his tablets and tried the changing lights exercise which helped to some extent.

We began to look at his life in general. It emerged that he had strong feelings about injustice, easily becoming anxious through his ability to empathise and suffer with others. He also felt annoyed if he thought anyone was insulting his intelligence by talking down to him.

We did some more NLP exercises, so he could disassociate himself more from his unhelpful feelings, and allow him to take a more detached view. Once again, we ended with hypnosis, when I added some new suggestions based on the new information revealed in the session.

The following week, Mark reported that for the first time in ages he had not suffered a migraine attack. He had also found the exercise in changing lights to be most effective and could do it with the utmost ease. He was feeling more positive in the mornings and finding it easier to live in the present moment. His concentration was also improving. He felt his mind had been opened.

We did three more sessions together, going into some detail about how he could continue to work on lesser issues to improve his life. The sessions showed he had taken great steps forward. At the fourth session, he reported that he could no longer remember how he used to feel in the morning, without putting himself into a trance first. He was unable to work the colour changes anymore (his mind knew they were no longer needed). He found the tape recording useful, not only for its content, but also as a soporific, he quickly dropped off to sleep using it. By now Mark was sleeping better and waking up feeling refreshed. He could relax his whole body at any time, no matter what was happening. Much of his stress had vanished, and the previous tension in his stomach had eased. Now, as soon as he began to feel tense he could go into a trance and feel better in seconds. Initially, it was frightening how quickly he could do this, but I reassured him that this was a common client reaction to feeling better. Even the most desirable of changes can be alarming when they are unfamiliar and make us feel different.

Mark finished working with me after five sessions. When I

later checked his progress, he confirmed that he was free of migraine and had stopped taking his medication. He was now eating whatever he liked with no adverse effects, other than a slight increase in weight. He was finding it easy to start whatever he had to do and no longer felt stressed. He had obviously learned the trick of living in the present and going with the flow.

Comments

It is interesting that these two remarkable success stories occurred simultaneously. Caroline and Mark share. many strong similarities:

• Both are optimistic, positive people who had overcome earlier difficulties in their lives.
• In both cases, good rapport was quickly established. Mutual trust is an important factor in good work.
• Both were exceptionally good at going into a trance.
• They sought help at the right time in their lives, when they were ready to change and to do whatever was necessary to achieve these changes.
•Both were willing to take an active part in treatment and 'doing therapy' for themselves.

Of course these cases are exceptional – negative passive clients are much harder to work with. Whenever I am stuck in my work, it helps to remember cases like these, and to recall that not everything is down to me. The essence of good work is effective co-operation.

Appendix

Selected bibliography

The aim of the selected bibliography is to give an overall view of the main ways of practising the different therapies used today (Windy Dryden's *Individual Therapy: a Handbook* is especially useful for this).

Some new developments relate to brief therapy (short-term treatment), the importance of the way we use language and how individual therapy must be seen in the context of the world we live in.

Eric Berne's *Games People Play* remains a best-seller, because the author has the rare gift of giving lots of vital information (about transactional analysis) in a way that is easy to read and entertaining.

The two books by Carl Rogers, *On Becoming a Person* and *Person to Person, the Problem Being Human,* give a clear picture of his ideas and stress the overwhelming importance of the nature of the relationship between therapist and client.

Deborah Tannen's two books *That's Not What I Meant* and *You Just Don't Understand* are easy to read and invaluable to people who have difficulty in communicating with others and for those involved in marital counselling.

Being Happy and *Making Friends*, the brilliantly illustrated Matthews' books, are great for humourously conveying all the important points about living a full life.

Beck A.T., Rush A.J., Shaw B.F., Emery G.,(1979),
Cognitive Theory of Depression,
The Guildford Press, New York.

Berne E., (1968), *Games People Play:
The Psychology of Human Relationships,*
Penguin, London (First edition 1964).

De Bono E., (1987), *Conflicts:
A Better Way to Resolve Them,*
Penguin, London (First edition 1985).

Dryden W. (edited), (1990).
Individual Therapy: a Handbook,
Open University, Milton Keynes.

Farrelly F., (1994), *Provocative Therapy,*
Meta Publications, U.S.A. (First edition 1974).

Freud S (1960) translated Strachey.,
Jokes and their Relation to the Unconscious,
Routledge & Kegan Paul, London.

Jung C.G., (1963), *Memories, Dreams, Reflections,*
Collins and Routledge & Kegan Paul, London.

Jung C.G. (1964), *Man and his Symbols,*
Aldus Books, London.

Matthews A., (1995), *Being Happy:
A Handbook to Greater Confidence and Security,*
Media Masters, Singapore (First edition 1990).

Matthews A. (1995), *Making Friends:
A Guide to Getting Along with People,*
Media Masters, Singapore (First edition 1990).

O'Connor J. & Seymour J., (1990, revised edition 1993),
*Introducing Neuro-Linguistic Programming: Psychological
Skills for Understanding and Influencing People*,
Aquarian, an imprint of HarperCollins, London.

Pain J., (1997) *So You Think You Need Therapy:
The Way to a Happier Life and Improved Relationships,*
Discovery Books, Great Britain.

Rogers C.R., (1990), *On Becoming a Person: A Therapist's
View of Psychotherapy,*
Constable, London (First edition 1967).

Rogers C.R., & Barry Stevens with Gendlin E.T., Shlien J.M.
& Van Dusen W. (1991), *Person to Person: The Problem
with Being Human,*
Condor, Souvenir Press, London (First edition 1967).

Rossi E., with Nimmons D.,(1991), *The 20 minute Break,*
Jeremy P.Tarcher, Inc., U.S.A.

Seligman M.E.P., (1995), *The Optimistic Child:
A Revolutionary Program that Safeguards Children
against Depression and Builds Lifelong Resilience*,
Houghton Mifflin, U.S.A.

Tannen D., (1992), *That's Not What I Meant!:
How Conversational Style Makes or Breaks your
Relations with Others*,
Virago Press, London (First published 1986).

Tannen D., (1992), *You Just Don't Understand:
Women and Men in Conversation,*
Virago Press, London (First published 1990).

Yapko M.D. (1997), *Breaking the Patterns of Depression,*
Doubleday, New York.

Useful addresses (UK)

British Association for Counselling
1 Regent Place, Rugby, Warwickshire CV21 2PJ
Tel: 01788 578328

British Association of Psychotherapists
121 Hendon Lane, Hendon, London N3 3PR

The Institute of Family Therapy
24-32 Stephenson Way, London NW1 2HX
Tel: 0207-391 9150

National College of Hypnotherapy & Psychotherapy
12 Cross Street, Nelson, Lancashire BB9 7EN
Tel: 01282 699378

Psychotherapy & Hypnosis Training Association
Regents College, Regents Park, London NW1 4NS
Tel: 0208 994 3580

Sensory Systems Training *(NLP courses)*
162 Queens Drive, Queens Park, Glasgow G42 8QN
Tel: 0141 424 4177

Tavistock Clinic
120 Bellsize Lane, London NW3 5BA
Tel: 0207-435 7111

United Kingdom Council for Psychotherapy (UKCP)
16 7-169 Great Portland Street, London W1N 5FB
Tel: 0207 436 3002

Useful addresses (International)

**World Council for Psychotherapy
and European Association for Psychotherapy (EAP)**
Rosenbursenstrasse 8/3/8, 1010 Vienna, Austria
Tel: 43 1 512 0444 Fax: 43 1 512 05 70
Email Wcp.office@psychotherapie.at

American Assoc. of Marriage & Family Counsellors
255 Vale Avenue Claremont, California 917711

American Counselling Association
5999 Stevenson Avenue, Alexandria, VA 22304
Tel: 703 823 9800 Fax: 703 823 0252

American Psychological Association
750 First Street Nt, Washington DC, 2002 4242
Tel: 202 336 5500

Australian Assoc. of Marriage & Family Counsellors
12 Payton Avenue, Dernancourt, S A 5075

Australian Institute of Professional Counsellors
PO Box 260, Lutwyche, Queensland 4030
Tel: 07 3857 2277 Fax: 07 3857 2644

Canadian Guidance & Counselling Association
00 220 Laurier Avenue West, Ottawa, Ontario, KIP 529
Tel: 613 230 4236 Fax: 613 230 5884

European Association for Counselling
PO Box 6699, Dublin 2, Eire
Tel/Fax: 00 353 1661 7279

Psychotherapy Society of Hong Kong
Contact Nia A Pryde, President
Tel: 852 2855 8435 Fax: 852 2872 7960

Irish Association for Counselling & Therapy
36/7 Lower Ormond Quay, Dublin 1
Tel: 353 (0) 1 230 0061

International Counselling Centre
Kobe Kasai Hospital, 11-15 Shinihara-Kitamachi 3
Chome, Nada-Ku, Kobe 657, Japan
Tel: 78 856 2201

Kenya Association of Professional Counsellors
PO Box 55472, Nairobi, Kenya
Tel: 786310 796283 575581

Kuwait University, Dept of Psychology
PO Box 23558, 1096, Kuwait
Contact Am Soliman

Malta Union of Professional Psychologists
PO Box 341, Valletta, Malta

New Zealand Association of Counsellors
17 Corokia Place, Manukau City, Auckland, NZ
Tel: 09 267 5973

The Albany Trust
Suite 18, Harley Chambers, 137 Cambridge Terrace,
Christchurch, NZ
Tel: 03 653 496
Contact Bridget Lee Nicoll

University Guidance & Counselling Centre
De La Salle University, 2401 Taft Amemce
D406 Hamla, Phillipines
Tel: 535 0226 Fax: 526 5915
E-mail: cedcpp@mail dku.edu.ph

UK Postal courses

Institute of Counselling
Clinical and Pastoral Department
6 Dixon Street, Glasgow G1 4AX
0141-204 2230

The Open University (OU)
Information office
Walton Hall, Milton Keynes, Buckinghamshire MK7 6AA
Tel: 01908 653743

National Extension College (NEC)
18 Brooklands Avenue, Cambridge, CB2 2HN
Tel: 01223 316644

Other titles from Discovery Books

So You Think You Need Therapy
The way to a happier life and improved relationships
by Jean Pain
ISBN 0-9518511-8-7
RRP £6.99

The Really Useful Guide to Natural Health and Beauty
by Catherine Beattie
ISBN 0-9518511-9-5
RRP £4.99

The Really Useful Guide to Supplements
by Catherine Beattie
ISBN 0-9518511-2-8
RRP £4.99

Forthcoming publications

Rosie's Armchair Exercises
A complete body workout from the comfort of your own armchair
by Rosita Evans
ISBN 0-9518511-7-9
RRP to be advised

The Good Spa Guide/Super Spas
Health farms and spas in Britain and Ireland
By Catherine Beattie
ISBN 09518511-5-2
RRP to be advised